PLANTS FOR GREENHOUSES AND CONSERVATORIES

RON MENAGE

CONTENTS

This edition published in 1989
by Octopus Books Limited,
a division of the Octopus Publishing Group,
Michelin House,
81 Fulham Road,
London SW3 6RB

ISBN 0 7064 3353 X
Produced by Mandarin Offset
Printed and Bound in Hong Kong

INTRODUCTION

There comes a point in every gardener's life when buying and planting is not enough – the ultimate challenge of starting from scratch is what thrills. That's when the greenhouse comes into its own.

Now there's no doubt about it, having a greenhouse or conservatory is like having a dog, and while you may not have to take it for a walk every day, you'll certainly have to cope with its daily needs. There'll be watering and feeding and pinching out and staking – none of which are what you'd choose to call stimulating.

But then there are the real jobs – sowing seeds of plants that have previously been just names in a book; taking cuttings from geraniums and fuschias that would otherwise perish outdoors during the winter, and trying your luck with something new every year.

Ron Menage has more experience of greenhouse gardening than most folk I know. He's tried all sorts of techniques and all sorts of plants and he knows which ones are worth the effort and which ones will probably lead to disappointment.

He'll help you choose the right greenhouse or conservatory for your needs and suggest ways of equipping it that will help to ensure you succeed with your plants, without spending every waking hour tending to their needs and worrying about their survival.

You may want a greenhouse to sit in among the flowers – more of a conservatory than a brightly lit workshop; or you may want to extend your harvesting season for fruits and vegetables. Whichever is the case, there is information here to make the dream reality.

All this can cost money, particularly if some form of special heating is involved, but, ever with an eye to reality, Ron Menage explains how to choose the right system for your needs, and how to run your plant factory as economically as possible.

I started my working life in a greenhouse, and quickly learned to appreciate the possibilities that such an environment could offer both plants and people. As far as plants are concerned the difficulty is in stopping them growing rather than starting them.

And the people? I've always found that the greenhouse is second only to the potting shed when it comes to escaping the furious bustle of everyday life and getting a bit of peace and quiet! That, coupled with the sight of ripening fruits and vegetables, and the scent of home-grown flowers makes the greenhouse a fine place to be whatever the weather. Try it and see.

GREENHOUSES AND CONSERVATORIES

The word 'greenhouse' describes a building used for a wide variety of horticultural purposes, including propagation, raising bedding plants, producing food crops, protecting tender plants over winter, and cultivating ornamentals. The word 'conservatory' on the other hand defines a place where decorative plants are displayed to please the eye.

Most conservatories are designed to be attractive structurally, both inside and out, and to be pleasant places where people can sit and relax. Ideally, they should be attached to a dwelling with a communicating door for easy access. They generally take the form of a lean-to. However, an ordinary free-standing greenhouse can be used instead in many cases.

Both greenhouses and conservatories can give enormous pleasure, and a greenhouse can also be a sound financial investment, soon paying back its cost in the form of produce. The weather protection it provides enables a vast range of plants from all over the world to be grown. Greenhouse gardening is a fascinating hobby that can be enjoyed all year round by both young and old.

A delightful conservatory in which to relax and enjoy a wide variety of plants all the year round.

A well-organized greenhouse is a source of both profit and pleasure.

TEMPERATURES

Much can be done without any artificial heating whatsoever. The protection from weather extremes that an unheated greenhouse gives is adequate for many plants and a glass structure traps enough free solar radiation to be warmer than outside for most of the winter. Providing enough heat to keep conditions frost free greatly widens your scope, and a minimum of about 4–7°C (40–45°F), 'cool house' temperatures, enables many subtropical plants to be grown. Temperatures above this can become rather expensive to maintain and are best provided for only small compartments, such as propagators, when required. Most of the plants dealt with in this book do not need high temperatures and are within the growing ability of most people.

SIZE AND STRUCTURE

Many people prefer to buy a prefabricated structure rather than build their own. Unless you are reasonably skilled in construction, this is by far the wisest procedure. There are now many types, sizes, and shapes available in a selection of materials. So it should not be difficult to suit individual requirements. The most popular size for a practical home greenhouse is about 3m × 2.4m (10ft × 8ft). However, if you can meet the expense, it may be worth buying something a bit larger, particularly if you do not plan to heat it; many almost hardy plants can become very large and will soon cry out for space. If you do plan to heat it, estimate the cost of fuel before buying. Some greenhouse designs can be extended by simply adding extra units as required. This is a feature to look out for when buying. Partitions with communicating doors can also be fitted to some. This means you can, for example, heat only a small section for greater economy, or provide a special environment for a particular group of plants.

Always buy from a reputable and, preferably, long-established firm. There are plenty of cheap greenhouses on the market, but they are likely to be a very poor investment. It is advisable to consult your local authority regarding planning permission before buying. This is particularly important if the structure is to be attached to a dwelling; there may be building regulations to comply with and often a low rate will be demanded. For small greenhouses, especially if they can be described as portable – that is, easily taken down and re-erected – there is rarely any regulation or rate requirement. Also check whether buildings erected on ground that is not your freehold become the legal property of the landlord.

GREENHOUSE DESIGN

Greenhouses come in a great many shapes and sizes, all with their own advantages and disadvantages. If you are thinking about buying one, it is a good idea to become familiar with the main types available, so that you end up with one that meets your requirements.

TRADITIONAL

This is the 'barn' or 'tent' shape. It forms a square or rectangle, with vertical sides and has a span roof with a central ridge. This design is still the most practical and allows the maximum utilization of available space. In some examples the ridge can be set off-centre to meet site requirements. This is usually known as three-quarter span. Nowadays it is not a common feature.

The roof should always have a good slope to shed any collected dirt, dead leaves and snow, for example. This applies to all greenhouse designs.

TUNNEL

This design is technically called 'curvilinear' and, with the exception of those made of plastic, is built of six or more panes of glass set in a continuous curve to give a 'tunnel' shape. For reasons described under Dutch light, this model allows excellent light entry, but suffers from the same disadvantages regarding lack of headroom and poor use of space.

CIRCULAR

These structures have at least six sides arranged to form a circle. They are by no means new – the shape was a favourite in Victorian times for conservatories. They were usually highly ornamental and there are models available today that will create the same atmosphere. A small circular greenhouse could be of special benefit to a disabled person, since most of it is easily accessible without much physical movement.

Below and right
The main types of greenhouse design.

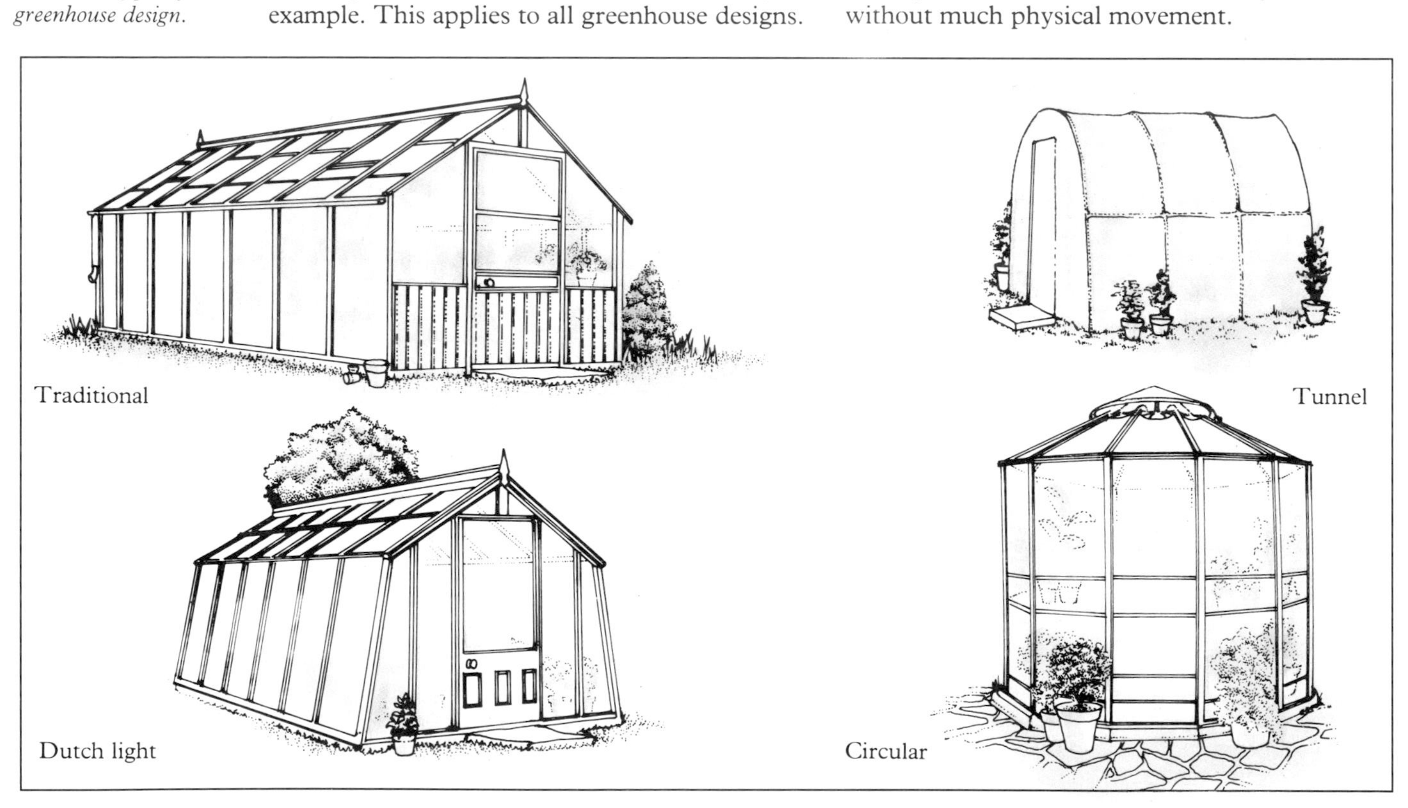

DUTCH LIGHT

This design has sloping sides. The idea is to set the glass as near as possible at right angles to the sun's rays so that light has a minimum thickness of glass to travel through and there is consequently minimum absorption. A pane of glass can absorb up to 20 per cent of light passing through it, even though it appears perfectly transparent to the eye. The Dutch light shape is of particular use to those growing winter crops, as the slightly increased light levels may give earlier maturation. However, sloping sides can be a nuisance: they make working close to the sides inconvenient and reduce headroom, and it may not be so easy to fit in taller plants or make as much use of the floor area as in traditional houses. Certainly, designs with sides set at a great angle should be viewed very critically.

Slanting sides can give greater stability to a structure, and this design should be given special consideration where the site is very windy or exposed to gales.

To the professional grower, the term 'Dutch light' also means a framed glass unit of specific size, used to make up frames or other structures. They are rarely employed by home gardeners.

DOME

The dome shape is a fairly recent introduction. It is made up of many triangular panes of glass supported by a strong metal framework. The effect is quite striking and futuristic. Light entry is excellent and the same advantages and disadvantages described under Dutch light apply. Better headroom around the sides can be obtained by mounting a dome on a low base wall. Domes make delightful conservatories and sun traps, but it's doubtful whether there's much point in using them for down-to-earth plant growing.

HIGH SOUTH WALL

This is another new introduction. It consists of two slanting sides of different heights, with a sloping roof between them. The taller of the sides is intended to face south or the direction with most light. Whether this has any advantage over conventional shapes is a matter of opinion.

LEAN-TO

This is a popular design with numerous special applications, and it's a favourite for conservatories, garden rooms, and sun rooms. It's also particularly suited to the cultivation of crops such as grapes and other fruits which can be trained against the rear wall. Lean-tos are usually set against brick walls at the side of a house or garage, but in some cases a tall weather-proof boarded fence would suffice. There is also a model which is half greenhouse and half timber garden shed. When set against a substantial wall, the greenhouse stays warmer overnight. Lean-tos are always the cheapest design to heat artificially.

Lean-tos can incorporate Dutch light sloping sides and such features as curved shapes and base walls. The type of environment offered by a lean-to, regarding light and warmth, depends on orientation (see page 9). Lean-to home extensions are rarely suitable as conservatories.

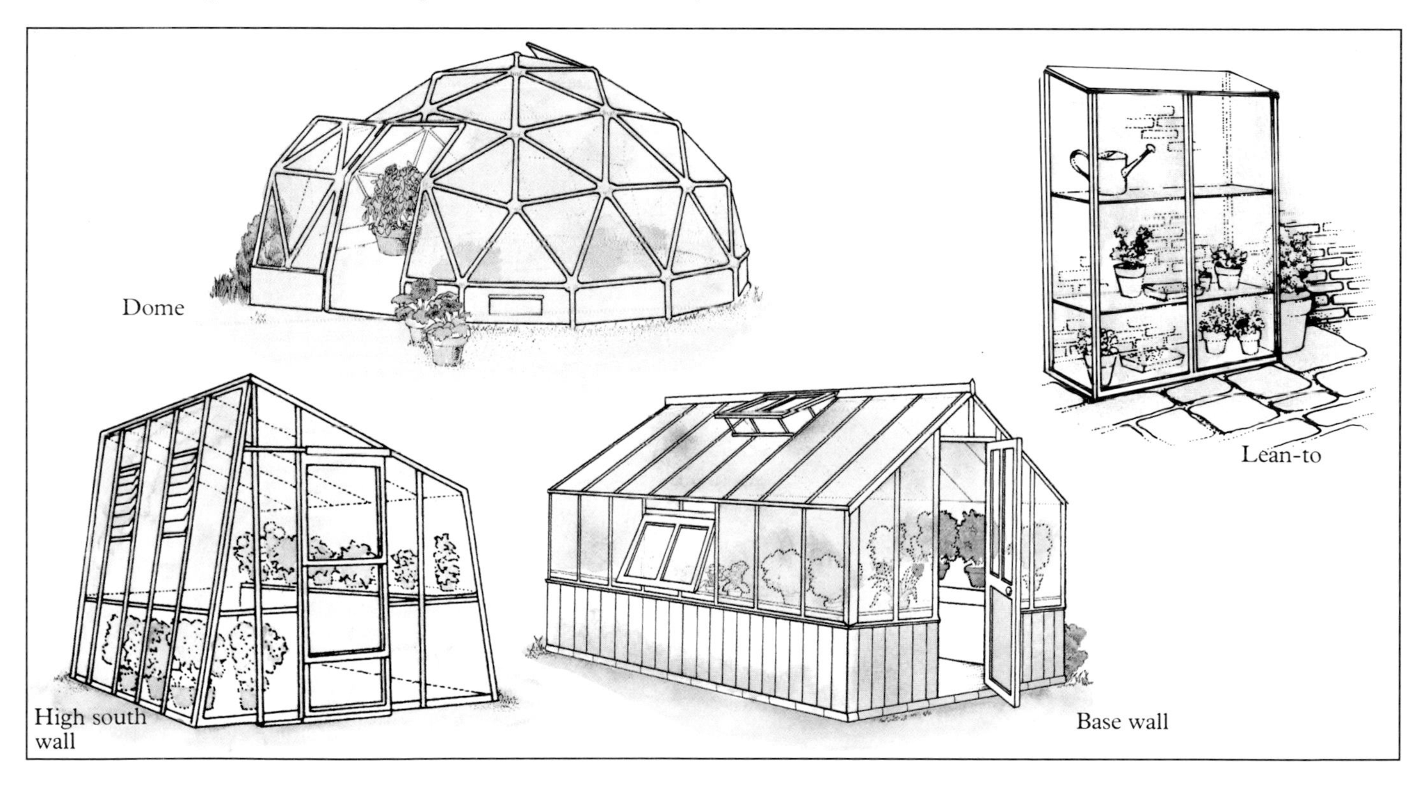

BASE WALL OR GLASS TO GROUND

Some greenhouse designs have timber-board or brick bases. Various forms of composition sheeting are also used, but asbestos is becoming less favoured for safety reasons. Base walls help to conserve warmth when a greenhouse is heated, but they obstruct sunlight and cut off a free supply of solar heat. A base-walled greenhouse is known as a 'plant house' and is usually fitted with staging to about the height of the wall for convenient working with potted plants. Space under the staging can be employed for those plants demanding less light. There are also designs with only partial base walling, the side admitting most light being left glass to ground. Some manufacturers produce models with removable base panels. These can be clipped on in the winter to conserve heat and removed in the summer months. Generally, a glass-to-ground house is the most versatile because of the amount of light admitted. It is easy to provide shade when wanted but no simple matter artificially to match the intensity of daylight. When a framework is designed to fit on to a brick or concrete base wall, it is best to have the base built by a professional bricklayer unless you are reasonably skilled.

SPECIAL DESIGNS

For some groups of plants, and for certain growing purposes, special designs of greenhouse are available. Some of the designs already mentioned would be suitable for some of these purposes. A glass-to-ground house is ideal for cacti and other light lovers, such as tomato plants and carnations. For perpetual flowering carnations, special carnation houses are made which give plenty of light, adequate height, and efficient ventilation. Base-wall greenhouses can be kept warmer and are hence suited to all particularly tender subjects, such as orchids and tropical pot plants. They are also useful for propagation needing moderate warmth. Designs with a base wall fitted with staging on one side, and glass-to-ground on the other, to accommodate tall light lovers, such as tomatoes, allow a wide range of plants to be grown happily in the same greenhouse. For alpines there are special greenhouses with plenty of ventilation and high staging to bring the dainty plants nearer the eye. These examples emphasize the importance of deciding what to grow before choosing a greenhouse. However, a purpose-designed greenhouse is not usually necessary. For example, various orchids, alpines, and other specialist plants will normally be quite happy in a mixed greenhouse if treated with reasonable care.

An alpine house needs a fresh, cool atmosphere with plenty of ventilation and light, as well as extra high staging.

CONSERVATORY DESIGN

Many of the basic comments made about greenhouse design also apply to conservatories. It has been pointed out that the lean-to is the favourite shape. If it can be sited where there is a direct communicating door giving easy access, a conservatory becomes almost an extension of the house. A design to blend architecturally with the dwelling is usually desirable. There are firms that can make reproduction ornamental structures if this would be more fitting.

Many ordinary 'greenhouse' lean-tos can be used as conservatories. Some people try to convert garden-room or home-extension buildings to conservatory use. But many of these have flattish roofs made of plastic which tend to collect dirt, dead leaves and the like, and need constant cleaning. They also exclude too much light, which limits the range of plants you can grow successfully.

If your house is a bungalow, be careful to check that any prefabricated structure you propose to buy is not too tall. The choice is often limited by the height of the house.

Lean-tos, designed for conservatory use, often have extra-wide sliding doors, allowing easy access to the garden. This is useful if you intend bringing in garden furniture or using the space as a patio extension. Some designs have partial or complete double glazing, others have curved glass pane eaves, an attractive feature which is now becoming popular. Structures with *toughened* glass are also available. This would be a wise choice where there are small children or elderly or infirm people. Where a conservatory is to be used for sitting out, as a place of relaxation, a design with a base wall may be preferred as it gives more privacy. The best conservatory design for a particular site is also, to some extent, governed by the direction in which it is to face (see page 9).

CHOICE OF SITE

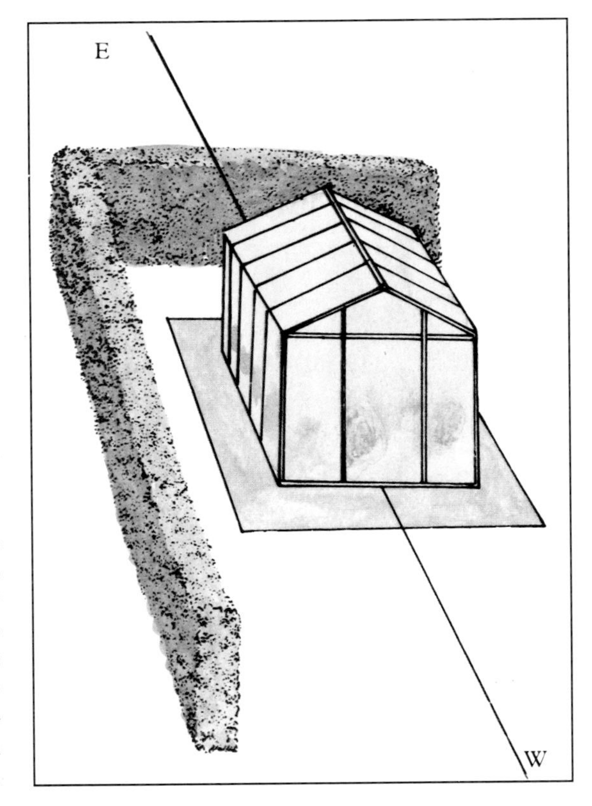

A rectangular greenhouse should be sited with the roof ridge running east-west and be sheltered from prevailing wind.

GREENHOUSE ORIENTATION

A square or rectangular greenhouse is best sited with its ridge, or length, running as near as possible from east to west. This gives maximum entry of sunlight in winter, when the sun is low in the sky, and hence maximum solar heat. In summer it is only necessary to shade the south side.

LEAN-TO AND CONSERVATORY ORIENTATION

The environment in a lean-to is greatly influenced by the direction it faces. A southern aspect gives the warmest and brightest conditions. In summer, shade must be given, or the greenhouse used for only warmth- and sun-loving plants. A north-facing lean-to tends to be chilly in winter, and is generally shady, but provides perfect conditions for most popular decorative plants, which prefer cool conditions. An eastern aspect warms up rapidly as the sun rises. A westerly facing lean-to gives warm conditions overnight. How a lean-to is used, therefore, obviously depends on orientation, and common sense should be applied in making the best use of the environment provided.

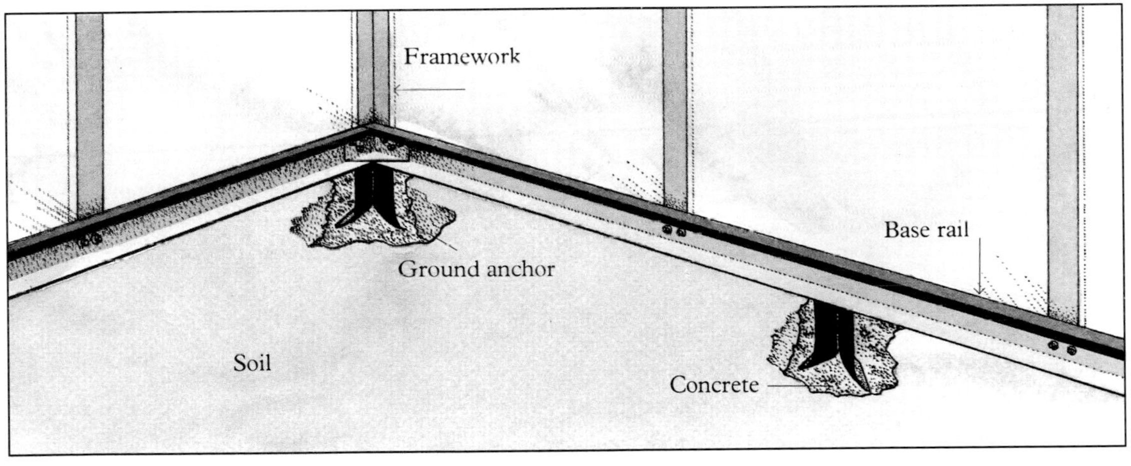

Ground-anchor system of foundation, in which alloy anchors bolted to the frame are concreted into the ground.

FOUNDATIONS

Suppliers of greenhouses usually recommend the most suitable form of foundation. When special kerbing is offered, this is a wise purchase. The ground must always be firm and level. Some modern alloy structures use a ground-anchor system. The frame is erected on firm level ground, and holes about the size of a bucket are dug at intervals around the base of the frame. Alloy anchors are then bolted on so that they drop down into the holes, which are then filled with concrete. This is the method most people find easiest to carry out. Another simple way to make a foundation for a *small* greenhouse, is to dig a trench about 150mm (6in) deep and 150mm (6in) wide to match the base size, and then fill it with a rather liquid concrete mix, which will find its own level.

It is worth taking trouble over constructing a sound foundation. If there is movement or subsidence after erection the glass may crack and the entire structure may have to be re-erected.

THE SITE

In a small garden there may be little choice of site for the greenhouse. For the convenience of running services, such as water, electricity or gas, a site near the dwelling house is desirable. An open, bright position should be chosen whenever possible. Avoid close proximity to large trees, especially evergreens. However, a wall, fence, or hedge, on the side of the prevailing wind and distant enough not to cast shade, makes a useful windbreak. Avoid wet and waterlogged ground, and places where frost is known to form.

STRUCTURAL MATERIALS

GLASS VERSUS PLASTIC

There is no doubt that, at present, glass is the best choice if a permanent long-lasting greenhouse is wanted. Glass has excellent solar heat trapping properties. You do not need to know much about the technicalities to appreciate this. Go into a glass greenhouse on a bright day when it's freezing outside and you will immediately feel the difference. In plastic structures the temperature can fluctuate widely with changes in weather conditions. With glass it's usually possible to maintain a steadier environment, and any artificial warmth provided is more easily retained.

Although some of the more rigid plastics are fairly long lived, none is as permanent as glass. Plastics have a tendency to become brittle with age, warp or crack, and some lose transparency or become tinted. Many plastics also look less aesthetically pleasing – they do not have that sparkling clarity. Plastics are also very soft compared with glass and soon scratch or become abraded by wind blown grit. Once dirt becomes ingrained, cleaning is difficult or impossible. There are a number of different types of plastic now used as glass substitutes. The best are, however, quite expensive.

A problem that arises with plastic is condensation. Water collects in droplets on a plastic surface and does not form a transparent film as it does on glass. The droplets may cut down light entry and raise humidity excessively. They can coalesce, producing annoying drips. Corrugated plastic roofs are particularly troublesome in this way. Despite this criticism, plastics do have their place and when used with common sense can be a better choice than glass in some cases.

An important property of plastic is safety. It may be a wise choice where there are small children or elderly people around or where structures are at risk from vandals. Plastics can also be used to partially 'glaze' a structure. They should be fitted where glass is most likely to break.

Plastic's lightness makes it easy to move and it is therefore useful in places such as a vegetable plot, where the entire structure can be moved as part of an annual crop rotation. Polythene houses are particularly useful in this respect. They are also convenient for crops that need little more than protection from the weather, or temporary accommodation.

Polythene and other plastics used for growing, must be of the ultra-violet light inhibited kind. This ensures maximum life when the plastic is exposed to sunlight. The letters 'U.V.I.' are what to look for. Even so, polythene is relatively short lived and must be replaced every two to three years. The best models are designed so that a new polythene cover can easily be slipped over a sturdy metal or timber frame.

Below *A light, easily portable and storable plastic greenhouse fitted on a sturdy frame.*

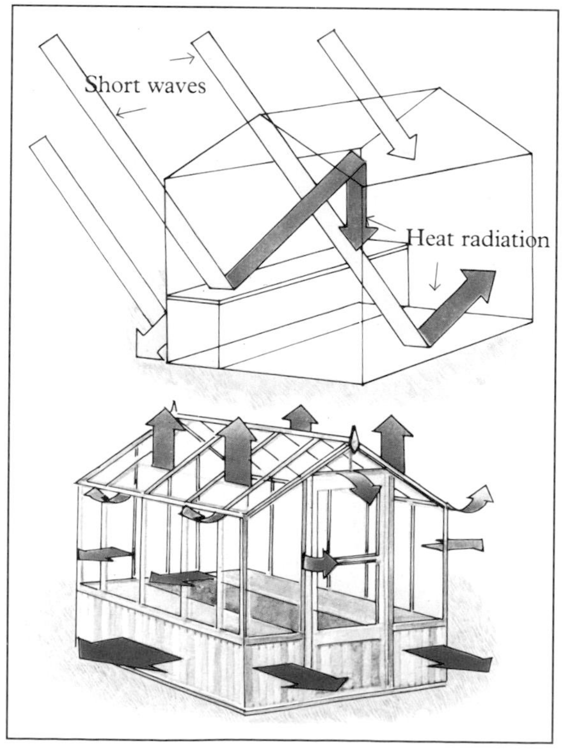

Top *Solar heat. Glass admits short waves; these change to heat radiation which is trapped.*
Bottom *Heat escape. Arrow size reflects rate.*

TIMBER FRAMEWORK

Timber is the traditional material and has been used for many years, but it has numerous disadvantages, such as its liability to rot or warp in a warm, damp greenhouse environment. However, timber has attractions: it's easy to work with, it's easily adapted and has a pleasing appearance. Its durability and the maintenance it needs depend on the quality and type of wood.

So-called western red cedar is reasonably priced, pleasing to the eye and remarkably resistant to rot, although *not* immune, as is sometimes suggested. It's advisable to have the framework chemically treated by the supplier before purchase, either with an anti-rot preparation or water repellant. All timber frames will need periodic painting or treating with preservative to keep them in good condition. For large greenhouses this can be inconvenient, expensive and time consuming. Be careful to use preservatives that are harmless to plants. *Never* use creosote.

Most traditional timber frames need linseed oil putty for glazing, although some special glazing mastics, which never set really hard, are to be preferred (see below). In some models the glazing bars are slotted and the glass merely slides in with no need of putty. This system produces a surprisingly watertight fit.

METAL FRAMEWORK

Metal greenhouses are often said to be 'cold' when compared with timber. It is true that metal is a much better heat conductor than timber but, since it's stronger, much less of it is necessary and more solar energy is therefore admitted. In fact, there is usually little thermal difference between timber and metal constructions except in houses with base walls, where there are large areas of unlagged metal. This should be strictly avoided. Large metal surfaces conduct away much valuable heat and become 'refrigerating' plates in frosty weather.

Although galvanized steel is sometimes employed, especially for the frames of polythene houses, the preference these days is for aluminium alloy. This material is extremely strong, and produces a framework that is light and easily transported. Erection is quick and simple, and dismantling, should the structure require removal at any time, is also easy. Aluminium alloy will not corrode, rust, rot, warp, or suffer attack by boring insects. It needs the minimum of maintenance and should retain its strength and quality for more than a lifetime.

If you don't care for the metallic appearance of alloy, you could buy a model in one of the newer white, green or bronze finishes. These look particularly good in conservatories. Unadorned metal will eventually form a dull grey coating that will protect the metal from further decay.

A timber-framed greenhouse of good quality wood can last well for many years but it will need some regular maintenance to keep it in good condition.

GLAZING

Glass should be of good quality and clear. For most general purpose glazing, it should be about 3mm thick (24oz/sq ft), but for some purposes it should be thicker or toughened, particularly where there is a greater need for safety, such as in conservatories. Where curved eaves are fitted, they should preferably be made from glass rather than plastic, although this is more expensive.

With a metal framework, linseed oil putty should *not* be used. A mastic that never sets hard, and hence allows expansion and contraction with temperature changes, should be employed, otherwise the glass is likely to crack. Many metal-framework houses now have glazing systems involving clips, strips, and plastic cushioning.

When glazing with putty or mastic, you need only bed the glass – do not put putty or mastic on top of the glazing bars as is done in domestic glazing. Also, you only need about 10mm (0.4in) of overlap between the panes. An excessive overlap collects dirt and algae.

A cross-section of one patent glazing system.

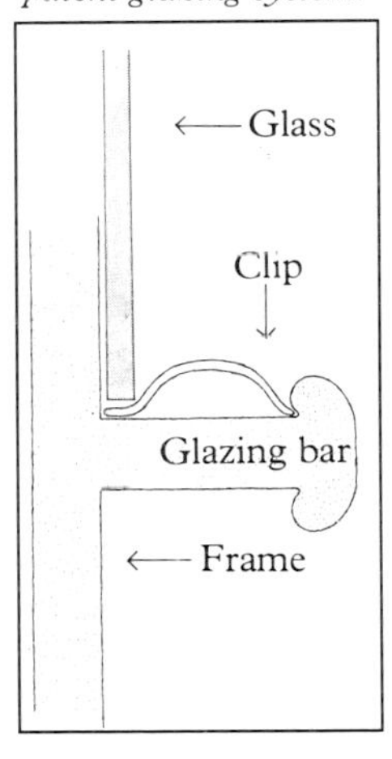

FEATURES TO LOOK FOR WHEN CHOOSING A GREENHOUSE OR CONSERVATORY

General strength and rigidity of frame
Strong ridge bar
Plenty of ventilators
Built-in guttering
Sliding doors
Good foundations – either kerbing or the ground-anchor system
Provision for the addition of an extension or partition
Well-fitting doors and vents – no gaps that might admit draughts
The roof, especially that of a lean-to, should have a moderately steep slope
Lean-tos designed for bungalows should be of the correct height

EQUIPPING A GREENHOUSE

Before a greenhouse is ready for use, a certain amount of basic equipment, such as ventilators and staging, has to be fitted. It is also worth thinking about automatic watering, and, if the greenhouse is to be used for raising tender plants, some form of heating.

VENTILATORS

The provision of ventilators is a matter that should be checked at the time of buying a greenhouse or conservatory; some suppliers consider them as extras. Most alloy greenhouses can be fitted with as many ventilators as you like. The basic number is usually included in the price. Always make sure that you have enough to ventilate the interior freely. It is better to have more than necessary; you do not have to open them all together, and a good distribution around the structure allows you to use them according to wind direction. The average 2.5 × 3m (8 × 10ft) greenhouse has at least two ventilators, one on the roof and one at the side; the number should be increased in proportion.

The conventional hinged ventilator with a stay bar is still used in most timber houses, but some designs incorporate sliding vents. Alloy structures are now being increasingly fitted with louvred vents but make sure these are tight fitting.

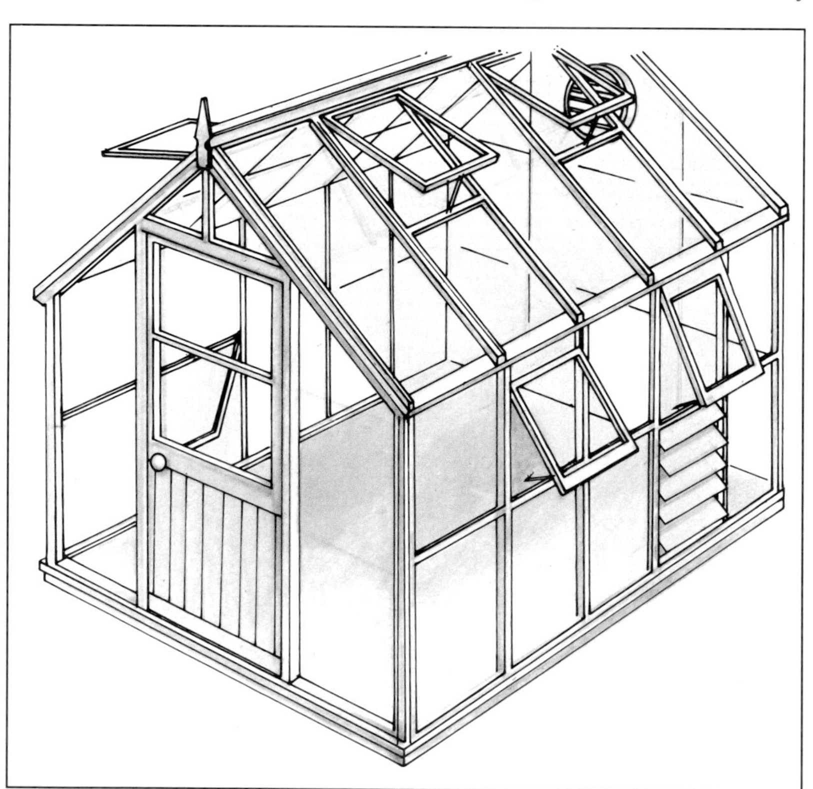

The ventilation system should be adjustable (and, ideally, automatic) to give the optimum effect in all weather conditions.

Ideally, the greenhouse ventilation system should be installed so that the roof ventilator is positioned as high up as possible, and the side ventilators are at ground level. This allows warm air to flow out freely at the top while cool air is drawn in from below. However, when there is staging or base walls, the vents are normally positioned just above them.

DOORS

Sliding doors are now often fitted to both timber and alloy structures, but the design of some leaves much to be desired. Metal doors can freeze up in winter and some have gaps which let in draughts. Doorways should be wide enough to allow free access for wheelbarrows or, in the case of conservatories, to admit plants in large pots or even garden furniture. Larger structures often have double doors. Sliding doors can be used as extra ventilators, since they are more easily adjusted than the hinged type. Where there are children, doors should be lockable for their safety.

GUTTERING

This is a highly desirable feature, since the constant shedding of rainwater around the perimeter of a greenhouse or conservatory can, in some cases, cause subsidence of the foundations because of the solvent action on the soil. The water can also seep inside, causing cold damp conditions. Many alloy structures are now equipped with built-in guttering, but, if not, plastic guttering is easy to fit to any type. The rainwater should be led away to a proper soakaway at a convenient distance from the greenhouse or conservatory or collected in a butt. This water can *not* be used for greenhouse irrigation. Today, we grow our plants in special composts which are clean and relatively sterile and to use rainwater collected from roofs is utter folly. It's a 'soup' of weed seeds, slimes, algae, pests, and diseases. Roofs can also collect weedkiller drift, which, even in trace amounts, can ruin greenhouse crops. (See page 19).

STAGING AND SHELVING

To make the most of space, some staging (benching) and shelving is needed. Sometimes this is at least partly supplied with a greenhouse and is included in the price, but it may be considered as an 'extra'. Timber greenhouses are often equipped with conventional slatted wooden staging. Alloy structures have metal supports topped with a variety of materials, including stout wire mesh on which pot plants are stood. In both cases shelving is generally of similar construction. Check that staging is strong enough to take a reasonable weight and that the greenhouse framework is similarly strong enough to support shelving laden with pots.

Staging should be covered with a layer of fine shingle or similar material to retain moisture during the summer months. This helps to maintain the right level of atmospheric humidity (see page 19). Slatted or mesh-topped staging will consequently have to be covered with polythene or some other suitable material to prevent the shingle falling through. Instead of shingle, capillary matting (see page 16) is often substituted. This holds moisture well and can be managed much more easily. In winter, it's desirable that any moisture-holding covering be removed to give dryer air conditions and encourage good air circulation. Slatted or mesh-topped staging can at this time be particularly beneficial.

Often it is useful to set staging along just one of the sides. A popular position is along the north side, leaving the south side free for tall plants. In many cases, modern staging is designed to be portable, and may also be adjustable for height and adaptable into different shapes and configurations. It is also available in tiered or stepped forms, for displaying plants in a conservatory, for example.

Above *Conventional slatted wooden staging and shelving. The staging should be covered in summer to help maintain the level of humidity.*

FRAMES

These are very useful adjuncts to the greenhouse, where they can relieve space for growing on the shorter plants. They can be used for the more hardy plants and for hardening off bedding plants (see page 51). Frames can be economically warmed with electric warming cables (page 15) and can be used inside the greenhouse for raising the temperature of a limited area. They make excellent large propagators treated in this fashion.

Whether they are used outdoors or in the greenhouse they are best situated with a northerly aspect, where they get little direct sunshine.

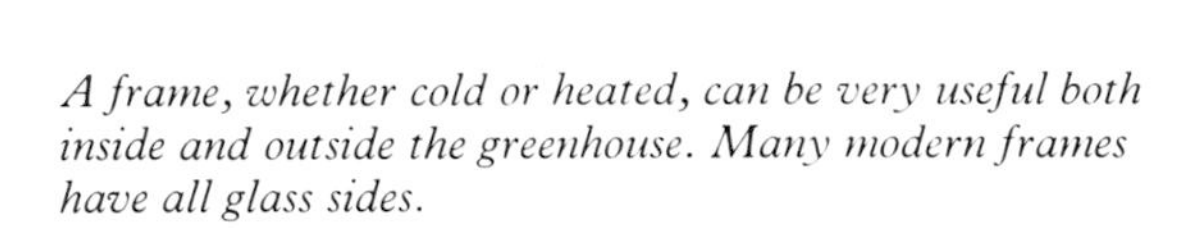

A frame, whether cold or heated, can be very useful both inside and outside the greenhouse. Many modern frames have all glass sides.

SERVICES

Electricity, water, and natural gas are all very useful in the greenhouse. In all cases the work of installation should be done in consultation with the authorities concerned and by professional contractors. Electricity is very useful for operating gadgets as well as for lighting and may be used for heating. Special fittings designed for safety in damp greenhouse conditions are available. A nearby supply of clean mains water, which can be used for automatic watering if desired, is also worthwhile. Natural gas is now becoming an important fuel for greenhouse heating.

CONSERVATION AND COST

The cost of raising the temperature of an average-sized greenhouse or conservatory to somewhere between frost free and 10°C (50°F) should not be prohibitively expensive. There are many ways in which heating costs can be kept to a minimum. A bright site will ensure maximum free solar heat. Shelter from excessive wind also cuts heat loss. It's essential to eliminate all sources of draught, such as gaps in the structure, ill fitting doors, vents, and glass. Except in some conservatory designs, double glazing is either very expensive or impractical for certain technical reasons. Lining with polythene is a simple and inexpensive way to achieve insulation that is almost as good. Clear polythene film, or preferably 'bubble' plastic which is sold specially for the purpose, will prevent at least 40 to 50 per cent of heat loss. It must be put up so that it encloses about 20 to 30mm (0.75 to 1.2in) of static air between the glass and the plastic. Special devices are available for fitting the plastic to metal framework, but on timber houses drawing pins can be used.

ASSESSING HEAT REQUIREMENTS

When installing heating equipment bear in mind that it must have a heat output to match heat loss when outside conditions are coldest. This can be roughly calculated from the size of the structure, the type and surface area of construction materials used, the minimum interior temperature desired, and the lowest outside temperature expected. Given these figures, suppliers of greenhouse heaters will recommend equipment with the most suitable rating in terms of British thermal units per hour, or wattage, in the case of electricity. It is most unwise to buy heaters without making this check first.

ELECTRICAL HEATING

This used to be considered expensive, but it must be remembered that there is virtually no waste and it involves the minimum of attention, and there is absolutely no contamination of the greenhouse atmosphere, which means ventilation, and therefore loss of heat, can be reduced considerably. Non-flued paraffin- and gas-heaters sometimes produce fumes, and there is always condensation and excessive humidity owing to the water vapour produced on the combustion of fuel. With these heaters, some ventilation must be constantly provided, to keep the air fresh and admit oxygen for the fuel's combustion. This means some waste of heat is inevitable, and therefore the fuel does not work out as cheap as might be supposed.

Electric fan heaters are very popular and give excellent distribution of warmed air. However, be sure to install a model in which the fan *and* the heater are both controlled by the thermostat. Models in which the fan runs all the time and only

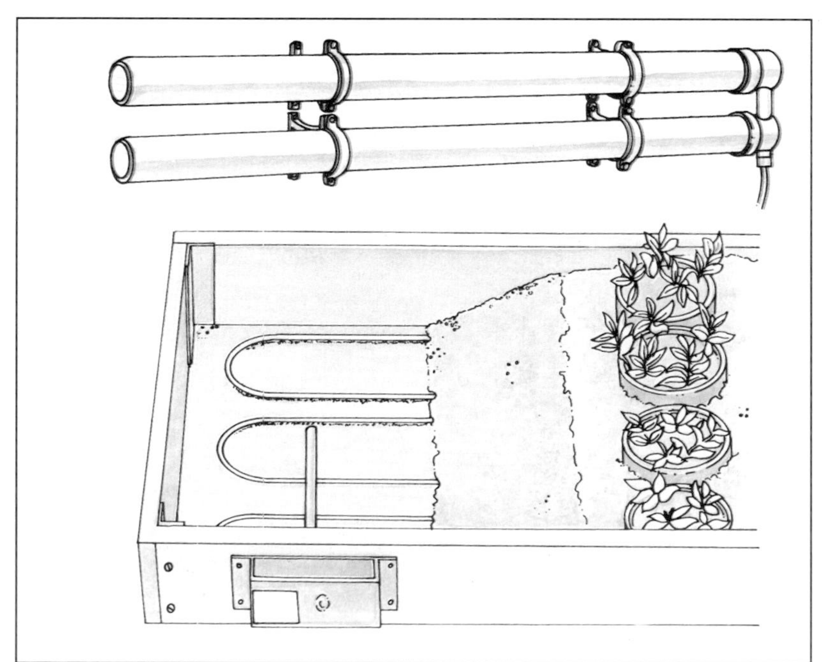

*Electrical heaters suitable for the greenhouse: tubular heaters (**top left**); soil-warming cables (**bottom left**); fan heater (**below**).*

the heater is thermostatically controlled are available, but in these the air continues to circulate after it has been warmed and consequently cools down more quickly. These systems are more expensive to run, but lining the greenhouse as described (see page 14) will reduce heat loss.

Tubular heaters are also favourites. They are best distributed evenly around the greenhouse and not banked all in one place. They are better positioned near the central pathway on both sides, than close to the greenhouse sides.

Convector heaters give moderate circulation of warmed air in the same way as fan heaters. Surprisingly, they are not often installed, but are nevertheless a good buy.

Warming cables have many uses. They can be used in beds or on limited areas of the staging to provide economical localized warmth. They are invaluable for gentle forcing of winter vegetable crops, and they can be used in frames or cases to warm small areas to a higher temperature than the greenhouse generally. This is especially useful for propagation. For the home greenhouse, special warming cables are sold. These should be used strictly according to the manufacturer's recommendations.

Only electrical heaters specially designed for use in the greenhouse should be used. Domestic equipment can be extremely dangerous in damp conditions and must not be used.

GAS HEATING

Piped natural gas is probably the cheapest fuel at present, and bottled gas the most expensive. Both can be used as fuel in the special greenhouse gas heaters that are now available. A high degree of thermostatic control is attainable with gas appliances, thus reducing heat waste. However, constant ventilation is essential. When the heater is not in operation and if weather permits the greenhouse should be freely ventilated.

PARAFFIN HEATING

The wick-type paraffin heater was at one time widely employed, but it is not easily controlled thermostatically and the fuel is expensive. Considerable waste is inevitable unless one is constantly at hand to adjust the wick according to weather conditions. Even so, this form is so reliable that it is a good idea to have an appliance at hand in case of an emergency, such as a breakdown in the main heating system or an exceptionally cold spell of weather.

If used as the main source of heat, the remarks made for gas regarding ventilation apply. Condensation is often excessive. Make sure you buy a properly designed greenhouse heater with adequate heat output. Check also that the BThU/hr rating is satisfactory. This is most important, since heaters are often purchased with outputs that are far too low. Gadgets for automatically topping up oil reservoirs are available, and these cut the chore of filling. The best type of greenhouse paraffin heater is a blue-flame type with a circular wick. It gives efficient combustion and is less liable to produce smells and fumes, provided you learn how to light the burner properly and obey the maker's instructions.

PIPED HOT WATER AND CONSERVATORY HEATING

Hot water pipes were often used at one time. They operate more efficiently where higher temperatures are required. They can be fuelled by solid fuel, oil, or gas. In conservatories or lean-tos, hot water heating can sometimes be run in from a domestic central heating system. It is essential, however, to consult a heating engineer beforehand to make certain the system can be extended.

Pipe heating is not now commonly employed for the average small home greenhouse. Even so, a modern boiler and equipment are much easier to install and operate than earlier types.

*Gas heater (**far left**) and paraffin heater (**left**), both designed for greenhouse use. Some constant ventilation is essential if either is used.*

Capillary matting is an excellent base for an automatic watering system. It absorbs and holds an amazing amount of water.

AUTOMATION

Thermostatic heating control is an important feature and should always be looked for, when buying equipment; the more accurate the thermostat the better.

There is now much automatic watering equipment on the market. One of the best systems employs special capillary matting which is kept constantly moist. This is spread over the staging and the plant pots are pressed on to it, uncrocked (see page 13), so that moisture can pass into the potting compost from the matting. Various trickle irrigation, overhead misting and spraying systems are also available but have more restricted, and sometimes specialized, applications. Generally, automatic watering is well worth considering, especially if you have to leave the greenhouse or conservatory unattended for long periods.

Ventilation can also be efficiently controlled by special greenhouse extractor fans operated by a thermostat. They should be of the type designed to prevent back draught. The size of fan, and the volume of air moved, depends on greenhouse size. Consult the supplier before buying and installing. Because fan-ventilated greenhouses are liable to dry out very quickly, some form of automatic watering or humidity control is a wise addition.

For the ordinary home greenhouse, automatic ventilator operators, controlled by temperature change, can be simply fitted. They need no electricity and require little attention. They are now very popular.

Automatic shading can be achieved using motor-operated blinds controlled by photo-electric cells. Unfortunately, this system is extremely expensive and is only used for special purposes.

GROUND SOIL, BEDS, FLOORS AND PATHS

SOIL SICKNESS

Crop rotation and the reasons for it are familiar to most schoolchildren. It is a practice followed by most outdoor gardeners – yet it is often promptly forgotten in the greenhouse. For the average small non-commercial greenhouse it's best not to use the ground soil for growing. Reasonably good results may be obtained for about two years or so, but after that what is known as soil sickness nearly always sets in. This condition produces serious plant deterioration due to a build up of excess unbalanced fertilizers, waste biochemical products from plant roots, and possibly pests and diseases. Under the cover of a greenhouse, where the soil is unexposed to weathering, 'sickness' soon becomes a problem, even if some crop rotation is carried out. Flooding the soil each year to wash out salts, sterilizing, or changing the soil, can help to overcome the trouble. But these measures are inconvenient, laborious, and rarely entirely satisfactory.

It is wise, therefore, to ignore the ground soil and grow everything in a suitable compost.

GREENHOUSE FLOORS AND PATHS

When the ground soil is not used for growing, a greenhouse can be erected almost anywhere on a sound flat surface. Concrete, asphalt, paving slabs, and the like make suitable floors. However, if there is no drainage, water may collect in puddles when the greenhouse is damped down (see page 19). Where a greenhouse is erected on soil, as is usually the case in the average garden, a simple effective floor can be made by levelling and firming the ground, and then strewing it with clean shingle or gravel, as used on driveways. This holds plenty of moisture during summer and will maintain atmospheric humidity without puddling. It is cheap and reasonably attractive.

Most small greenhouses are given a central path but, in houses more than 3m (10ft) wide, there is usually room for an additional central run of staging with a path on both sides.

CONSERVATORY FLOORS

Most people prefer a conservatory floor to be decorative or at least to be in keeping with the surroundings. Whatever is used should be unaffected by water, although, in conservatories, damping down is done with more care and discretion. Vinyl flooring, as used in domestic kitchens (but not cushion backed) lasts well provided it's put down on a perfectly smooth surface. Special self-levelling surface mixes for application to concrete bases are available. Ceramic floor tiles can be used, but plastic flooring tiles are liable to lift if water gets under them.

BEDS

Where beds or borders are wanted in greenhouses or conservatories, dig trenches of the required size and depth and remove the soil. Line the trenches with polythene sheeting. Make slits at intervals for drainage and fill with a suitable compost (see page 18). Raised beds or borders can be made similarly by draping polythene over a frame of boards of the required height. The polythene isolates the compost from the ground soil so that it cannot become contaminated, and the more restricted volume of compost is easier to replace. It is also easier to maintain a better fertilizer balance. Electric warming cables can be used in the beds to provide localized warmth. Beds and borders such as these can be filled with peat for the display of ornamentals. The plants are left in their pots and plunged to just over their rims. This also allows plants to be easily changed about according to the season. You should always try to arrange them in an attractive way, especially when using the beds and borders for display. Raised beds could be of special benefit to some disabled people.

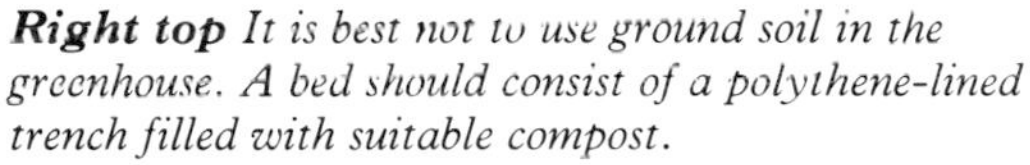

Right top *It is best not to use ground soil in the greenhouse. A bed should consist of a polythene-lined trench filled with suitable compost.*
Bottom *Slatted exterior blinds are best for shading.*

SHADING

Nearly all greenhouses need shading at one time or another. An unshaded structure in a bright position can become so hot in summer that all the plants will be severely damaged or even killed. Blinds and special paints for application to the exterior glass are employed. The former can be expensive but are usually preferred for conservatories. For this purpose, slatted exterior blinds are best. Flimsy blinds of plastic or textile are liable to blow away in a strong wind. Interior blinds may give protection from direct sun scorch, but do little to keep down temperature.

Shading paints can be difficult to apply and to remove. However, a recently introduced electrostatic type, sold under the name Coolglass, is much easier to handle. It is a powder and mixes instantly with water. It can be sprayed or brushed on and is quite fast, even in torrential rain; yet it wipes off easily with a dry duster.

THERMOMETER

To help maintain the correct temperature in a greenhouse, a maximum and minimum thermometer should be installed. This type of thermometer has indicators which record the lowest and highest temperatures reached since the thermometer was last set. This is useful to show the temperature range in your absence. There are various designs. It is a small item – but a vital piece of equipment for proper management of greenhouse temperature. If you have separate sections, each needs its own thermometer.

FLOWERING AND FOLIAGE PLANTS

It is vital to choose plants that are suitable for growing in the temperature and light conditions of your greenhouse or conservatory. If you do not mix plants with very different requirements, for example, succulents, which need plenty of light, and ferns, which need shade and moisture, you will obtain far better results. It may, however, be possible to suit individual needs to some extent by putting plants which require shade under staging, for instance.

Buy plants only from reputable suppliers. Make sure they are healthy and correctly identified and labelled. There are specialist nurseries for some types of plants but many others can be grown successfully and cheaply from seed (see page 50).

COMPOSTS

Never use garden soil for pot work nor, in most cases, the greenhouse ground soil (see page 16). The use of unsterilized garden soil and crude fertilizers, such as animal manures, is inviting failure and disappointment; all manner of pests and diseases can be introduced.

There are a number of proprietary seed and potting composts available from which to choose. These are mostly peat based, are free from pests, disease and weed seed, and have an ideal fertilizer balance. The John Innes composts, which are loam based, are also a good buy provided they are made exactly to the original formulae set by the John Innes Horticultural Institute.

When a lot of compost is needed, it is cheaper to make up a peat and grit mix yourself and add a ready-mixed fertilizer concentrate, available with full instructions from garden shops. Such DIY composts can be made up with very little effort in a few minutes. The John Innes composts have more complicated ingredients, including special loam, and DIY preparation is, therefore, not often attempted.

POTS AND POTTING

Plastic pots are now widely used. They are lightweight, easy to store and clean, and retain moisture better than clay so the compost does not dry out so quickly. Clay pots, being porous, are a better choice when plants need to be plunged in a moisture-retaining material (see page 17).

Pot sizes mentioned in the text are all average. When potting most decorative plants, use a pot just large enough to take the plant comfortably. As it grows, the plant needs to be potted-on. This means transferring it into successively larger pots as the roots fill the existing one. Tap the plant out of the container, if there's a mass of tangled roots encircling the pot, the plant is 'pot bound' and should be put into a slightly larger container with fresh compost. This ensures that the roots always have a supply of 'sweet' compost with the right balance of nutrients. Exceptions to this treatment are plants known to be fast growers and vigorous. These, which include certain vegetable crops, can be given larger pots in the early stages.

Obviously, after a time, plants cannot be potted-on any further. If they are perennial, they can simply be repotted. This means removing the plant from its pot, carefully reducing the size of the root ball, teasing away old roots and compost, and potting back into the same sized pot with fresh compost. You should do this just before the plant is expected to make new growth.

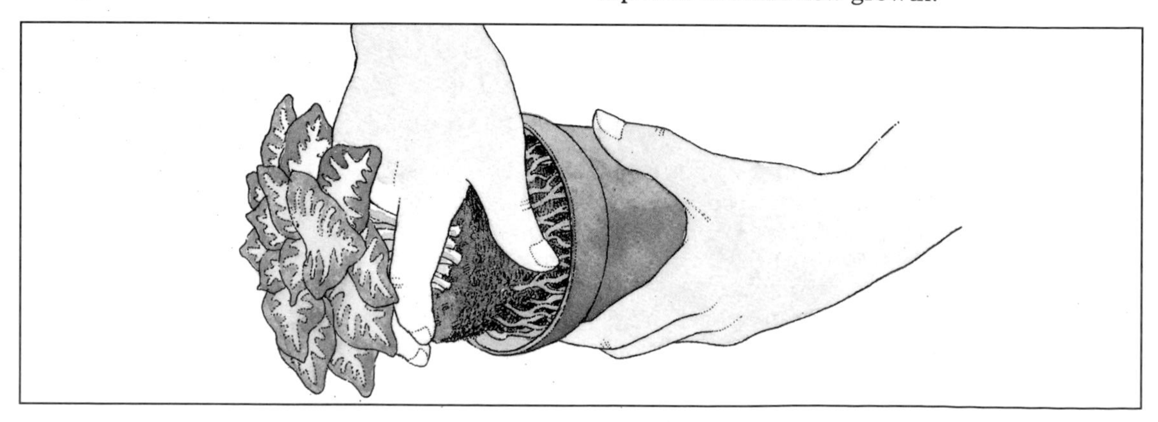

When potting on, pass the fingers of one hand, palm down, around the base of the plant, turn the pot upside down and tap the pot then gently pull it away.

Another method for plants in final pots is to top dress. This means removing the upper layers of compost and replacing them with fresh. Alternatively, mix in some balanced fertilizer at the top of the pot. Nowadays, the excellent systemic and foliar feeds available make the feeding of established plants easier and top dressing less important than it used to be.

When potting, always leave a space between the surface of the compost and the top of the pot. This is the watering space. It assures water penetration and helps to assess the amount needed.

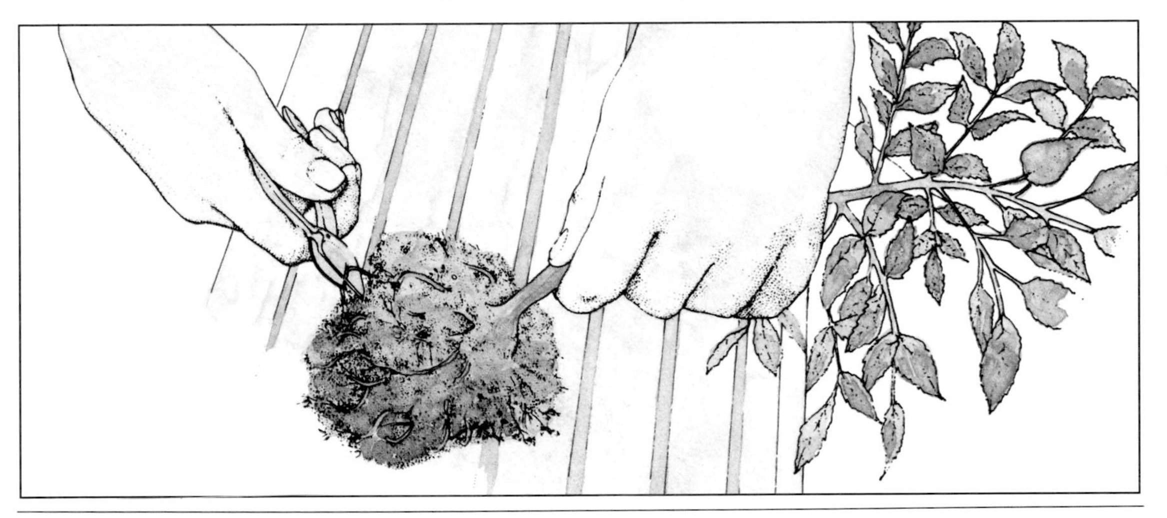

When repotting a mature plant, reduce the size of the root ball before potting back in the same size pot with fresh compost.

CULTURAL CARE

DAMPING DOWN

This entails sprinkling water over as much of the floor and staging as is convenient. Evaporation of the water then causes cooling and increases humidity which growing plants like. A moist atmosphere also means that they need less frequent watering. Damping down must not be done in winter. The air then should be kept on the dry side since too much humidity encourages moulds and mildews when conditions are cool.

WATERING

Always use *clean* water. Rainwater collected from roofs and stored in dirty butts should never be used as it is likely to be contaminated. Most plants will be far healthier with tap water. In areas where this is 'hard', plants disliking lime can be watered with clean rainwater collected in bowls. However, it is doubtful if this is really necessary provided that such plants are grown in special lime-free 'ericaceous' composts, which are available from garden shops.

The best general rule for watering plants is to keep the roots constantly moist. It is vital to avoid absolute dryness or waterlogging. Water must also be given according to a plant's needs and not in standard doses. When plants are dormant, as in winter, little if any water is required. Wet conditions then will lead to rotting and possibly to cold damage. In summer, however, water may be needed frequently: vigorous plants may require watering several times a day.

In general, plants need more water when conditions are warm and bright than when they are cold and dull. The best time to water is in the morning. Erratic watering leads to wilting and bud, flower or leaf shedding. Overwatering is often indicated by a sickly appearance, poor growth and yellowish foliage.

FEEDING

The rules given for watering also apply to feeding. Feed according to a plant's needs and vigour. When a suitable potting compost is used, feeding is not necessary until the plant is in the final pot. Feeding can be done with proprietary feeds which contain the nutrients in the correct, scientifically balanced proportions. These should be used according to the instructions on the label. Using DIY mixes, hit and miss fertilizers, or crude manures is most unwise. Overfeeding is harmful and you should never exceed the recommended doses. Frequent feeding with weak solutions gives the best results. Do not feed when the roots are dry. Foliar feeds, which are sprayed onto the leaves, can give a quick improvement. Some contain plant vitamins and hormones.

TEMPERATURE CONTROL

Make every effort to ensure that the temperature does not fall below the minimum required by your plants in winter. Thermostatic control of artifical heating usually makes management easy. In summer, conditions must not be allowed to become too hot. Damping down, shading with a white compound (such as Coolglass) and careful use of ventilators enables temperature adjustment. Excessive heat can prevent some plants from flowering. Erratic temperature changes lead to bud shedding and physiological problems.

Abutilon

GROWING FROM SEED

The cheapest way to acquire plants is to grow them from seed. Look through the catalogues from the leading seed firms and you will find an exciting and extensive range to choose from. There are always lots of seed novelties on offer as well as the more popular bedding plants, many of which make fine pot plants.

Some people think that starting from seed is a slow and difficult way to begin. This is not true, and if you follow the techniques given in chapter 5 success can be assured.

Calceolaria

Exacum affine

PLANTS TO GROW FROM SEED

Plant	Description/Cultural Hints	Final Pot Size	Min. Temp.	Germination Temp.
Abutilon	Indian mallow. The hybrids have a neat habit with large cup-shaped, veined and richly coloured flowers in the same year as sowing; flowers in winter if frost free. Grow the hybrid 'bella'.	130mm	5°C	16–18°C
Asparagus sprengeri	Foliage plant with trailing stems of fine needles; good for hanging baskets. *A. plumosus* has very fine needles and a spreading habit. It is popularly called the asparagus fern. Easy to grow.	180mm	5°C	18–21°C
Begonia	The fibrous-rooted bedding begonias make fine pot plants, with masses of flowers in many colours and glossy attractive foliage. They may also flower in winter, given a bright position.	130–180mm	10°C	18–21°C
Browallia	Sow the dwarf variety 'Troll' in March to give masses of blue or white cup-shaped flowers in autumn and winter. Discard after flowering.	130mm	10°C	18–21°C
Calceolaria	Slipper flower. A great favourite with a profusion of pouch-shaped flowers in dramatic colours, often speckled. Sow May to June for Christmas-to-spring bloom. F1 hybrids bloom earliest. Keep frost free over winter.	130mm	5°C	16–18°C
Capsicum	Ornamental shrub bearing orange to red berries, usually elongate in shape, between summer and Christmas. Easy to grow. Discard when berries shrivel.	100mm	5°C	18–24°C
Catharanthus rosea (Vinca)	Dainty evergreen shrubby perennial with eyed flowers in white to carmine. Dislikes chill.	130mm	10°C	16–18°C
Cineraria	Very popular neat plant smothered with daisy-like flowers in rich colours, often zoned with white. Can be grown with calceolarias.	130mm	5°C	16–18°C
Coleus	Beautifully coloured foliage plants; now available in many forms including miniatures. Sow February to March for summer/autumn display. Not worth trying to save over winter.	100–130mm	5°C	16–18°C
Cuphea ignea	Mexican cigar plant. Sow February/March. Neat bushy plant smothered with small red tubular flowers from summer to autumn. Discard after flowering.	130mm	5°C	18–21°C
Cyclamen	Popular winter-flowering plant with shuttlecock-shaped flowers. Takes about 14 months to flower from seed; sow November and maintain a steady temperature.	130mm	10°C	16–18°C
Eucalyptus	*E. citriodora*, with lemon-scented, spear-shaped foliage is best for pot cultivation. This species dislikes chill. Can be grown in 130mm pot for several years.	130mm	10°C	18–24°C
Exacum affine	Short, compact plant with small purplish flowers. It is grown mainly for its scent, but note not all varieties are fragrant. Sow February/March for late summer/autumn bloom. Grow several seedlings in a 10cm pot. Discard after flowering.	130mm	5°C	18–21°C
Fatsia japonica	Foliage plant with large glossy palmate leaves. Good for cold conditons. Will eventually grow very large; can then be put outdoors.	180mm	5°C	18–24°C

PLANTS TO GROW FROM SEED

Plant	Description/Cultural Hints	Final Pot Size	Min. Temp.	Germination Temp.
Geranium	Popular name for zonal pelargoniums. Several excellent hybrids can be grown from seed. F1 hybrids are especially recommended. Sow January/February for flowering the following summer. Plants can be saved and propagated from cuttings. See page 30.	130mm	5°C	22–23°C
Gerbera	Grow the variety 'Happipot' which has a dwarf habit and large daisy-like flowers in lovely colours. Sow February/March for summer/autumn bloom.	150mm	5°C	18–21°C
Grevillea robusta	A graceful foliage plant with 'ferny' foliage. Excellent for cool conservatories. Pot into a lime-free (ericaceous) compost. Can become rather large after a few years.	170mm	5°C	18–24°C
Heliotropium peruvianum	Heliotrope. Shrubby plant with wrinkled mid- to dark-green leaves; sometimes known as cherry pie. The variety 'Marine' has flattish heads of purplish flowers with powerful fragrance. Sow February/March for summer/autumn bloom. Cut back after flowering and save over winter in frost-free conditions.	130mm	5°C	18–21°C
Hibiscus	Grow the variety 'Southern Belle' which has exciting flowers the size of dinner plates, coloured white to carmine. Sow February/March for summer/autumn blooms. Discard after flowering.	250mm	5°C	18–21°C
Hypoestes phyllostachya	Polka-dot plant. Foliage plant with pink spots on olive-green, pink flushed foliage. Grow the variety 'Pink Splash'. Sow February/March for summer onwards. Pinch back frequently. Discard when plant becomes straggly.	100mm	5°C	18–21°C
Impatiens	Busy-lizzie. Extremely popular ornamental plant bearing a profusion of flowers in bright colours. Choose low compact varieties for pots. Sow March to bloom from summer onwards. Will flower in winter with moderate warmth. Sow afresh when plants deteriorate.	100–130mm	5°C	21–24°C
Ipomoea	Morning Glory. Annual climber with beautiful large convolvulous flowers. Variety 'Heavenly Blue' is a favourite; other colours are available. Climbs to 2.4m (8ft). Give a bright position.	180mm	5°C	20–24°C
Jacaranda mimosaefolia	Foliage plants with graceful 'ferny' appearance, ideal for conservatories. May become too high for limited space in a few years.	250mm	5°C	18–24°C
Lagerstroemia indica	Neat perennial shrub with unusual white, pink, or reddish flowers. Keep dryish after the leaves are shed in winter. Grow dwarf hybrids.	150mm	5°C	18–21°C
Lantana	Verbena-like flowers in various colours, changing as they age. Grow hybrids with neat shrubby habit.	150mm	5°C	21–24°C
Lobelia tenuoir	Large blue-flowered greenhouse annual lobelia. Dislikes chill. Put several seedlings to each 130mm pot.	Several seedlings per 130mm pot	5°C	16–18°C
Mimosa pudica	Sensitive Plant. A foliage plant with delicate foliage folding up when touched. Grow as an annual.	100–130mm	5°C	18–21°C
Nemesia	Dwarf garden hybrids, make good pot plants. The variety 'Fire King' has rich red shades.	Several seedlings per 130mm pot	5°C	16–18°C
Nierembergia	Low-growing perennial with campanula-like purplish flowers. Keep dryish after the leaves are shed in winter. Grow the variety 'Purple Robe'.	130mm	5°C	16–18°C

Heliotrope

Morning glory

Nemesia

Plumbago

African violet

Butterfly flower

PLANTS TO GROW FROM SEED

Plant	Description/Cultural Hints	Final Pot Size	Min. Temp.	Germination Temp.
Petunia	Most are suitable for hanging baskets; the double forms are useful for pots. Give a position in bright light or, under glass, flowering may be poor.	3–6 seedlings per 130–180mm pot	5°C	18–21°C
Phlox drummondii	Can be sown in autumn for early spring display as well as given usual half-hardy annual treatment. Grow the dwarf compact varieties.	3 seedlings per 130mm pot	5°C	16–18°C
Plumbago capensis	Attractive perennial wall shrub with beautiful blue phlox-like flowers. There is also a white form. Flowers two years after sowing. Size can be restricted by pruning back after flowering.	250mm	5°C	18–21°C
Polyanthus	Choice of many varieties; innumerable colours. Sow February/March for winter to spring flowering. Ideal for cold conditions.	130mm	5°C	16–18°C
Primula malacoides	Fairy Primula. Whorls of flowers in various colours, borne above a neat leaf rosette. Sow May for following spring bloom. This species does not cause skin rash like *P. obconica* and *P. praenitens.*	100–130mm	5°C	16–18°C
Ricinus	Caster oil plant. Annual foliage plant. Grow 'Impala' with rich maroon-tinted glossy foliage and reddish seed capsules. Sow February/March. The seeds are poisonous.	130mm	5°C	18–21°C
Saintpaulia	African Violet. Popular houseplant. Needs moderate steady warmth. Transfer indoors during winter. Grow F1 hybrids, such as 'Blue' and 'Pink Fairy Tale', which are vigorous and easier to manage. Sow February/March.	130mm	5°C	21–24°C
Salpiglossis	Glorious trumpet-flowered annuals with rich colours and exotic veining. Sow February/March. Pinch out seedlings to encourage bushy growth. Can also be sown autumn for flowering following early spring. Grow hybrids 'Splash' or 'Ingrid'.	1–3 seedlings per 130mm pot	5°C	18–21°C
Schefflera	There are several species of different heights. Large pale green, shiny palmate foliage with a tropical look. Good for the cool conservatory.	180mm	5°C	18–24°C
Schizanthus	Butterfly Flower. Dainty 'ferny' foliage and masses of pretty butterfly flowers with many colours and markings. Sow February/March for summer flowering. Giant hybrids can be sown in autumn for spring flowers. Pinch out seedlings of tall forms only to promote bushy growth. Keep frost free over winter. The dwarf varieties are easy to grow as annuals.	Several seedlings per 130mm pot	5°C	16–18°C
Solanum	Winter Cherry. Popular winter and Christmas pot plants with bright cherry-sized red berries. Sow February. Stand outside while flowering to set fruit. Plants can often be saved if cut back when berries shrivel.	100–130mm	5°C	18–24°C
Streptocarpus	Cape primrose. Profusion of trumpet flowers on wiry stems in delicate colours. Sow February to flower same year. Keep frost free and only slightly moist during winter.	130mm	5°C	18–24°C
Thunbergia alata	Black-eyed Susan. Dainty annual climber with orange, cream, or white flowers, often with a jet black 'eye'. Sow February/March to flower from summer onwards. Train up canes. Can also be used to trail from hanging baskets.	130–180mm	5°C	18–21°C

GROWING FROM BULBS, CORMS AND TUBERS

The word 'bulb' is often used by the layman to include corms, tubers, rhizomes, and similar items which are known as 'storage organs' by the botanist. These storage organs all contain food, which ensures the plant gets a good start in life. When you buy them, look for high quality, since their performance depends on how well they have been produced.

Always purchase from a reputable firm. Do not accept anything soft and spongy or showing signs of rot or mildew. Small size is also best avoided, since it may indicate that the organ is not developed enough to produce flowers.

COMPOST, POTTING AND GENERAL CULTURE

Always use a proper potting compost (see page 18). Choose a pot of suitable size for the particular bulb. Small bulbs can be grouped, large bulbs need individual pots. Most bulbs grown for the greenhouse can be potted shallowly with their tips protruding well above the compost surface. This gives plenty of room for the roots in the pot. Decorative bowls are popular for growing bulbs in, but take care as these may become waterlogged if there are no drainage holes.

Position the bulbs on a layer of moist compost.

HARDY AND TENDER GROUPS

Plant storage organs fall into two categories: hardy and tender. The treatment of each is quite different. The hardy group includes the popular, well-loved spring-flowering favourites such as daffodil, hyacinth and crocus. These are indispensable for unheated or cold conditions. The tender group includes many of the greenhouse 'exotics', for example, gloxinia, begonia, and hippeastrum, which require warmer conditions.

GROWING THE WINTER TO SPRING FLOWERING GROUP (Hardy)

The great majority of these should be potted from August to October. After potting they should be plunged in moist peat or grit, outdoors, to give about 150mm (6in) covering. The plunge must be kept moist but protected from rain to prevent waterlogging. On no account keep the containers in a warm place. Leave them in the plunge for about six to eight weeks. The bulbs should by then have made plenty of roots and can be brought into a cool greenhouse or conservatory and gradually introduced to full light. Too much warmth is harmful to this group and may cause weak, lanky growth and failure to flower.

GROWING THE SUMMER TO WINTER FLOWERING GROUP (Tender)

These are potted or started into growth in gentle warmth from early to late spring. Those storage organs without an obvious growing point, such as gloxinia and begonia, should be just covered with moist peat in a warm propagator. Inspect them daily and, as soon as you can see roots or shoots, pot into a suitable potting compost. Again they need only be potted at a shallow depth. Most of this group require a minimum temperature of about 10°C (50°F) and will grow faster if it is a few degrees higher. Keep the atmosphere moist and protect from direct sunlight.

TREATMENT AFTER FLOWERING

Plants of the hardy group can be put outdoors in any convenient place. Continue to water and feed them until the foliage dies down naturally, this is important to their flowering in future years. The bulbs often multiply and may need separating and repotting in the future.

The tender group should also be watered and fed until the foliage shows signs of deterioration, and then allowed to become dry. When dry, tip out of the pots, free from compost, remove stem and leaf vegetation, and store dry in clean sand in a frost-free place over winter. Delicate or brittle storage organs, such as some rhizomes and tubers, can be left in their pots, which should be turned on their sides until next repotted.

PREPARED BULBS

This term is used to describe bulbs and other storage organs that have been specially temperature treated to induce early or out-of-season flowering. The suppliers' instructions should be closely followed regarding cultivation and temperature. The temperature stated is sometimes initially rather high and may not be practical to attain in an ordinary greenhouse. The forcing can then be done in a warm room indoors. When approaching flowering, move the plants to the cooler conditions of a conservatory.

Anemone

Crocus

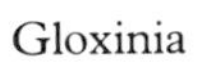
Gloxinia

COLOURFUL BULBS, CORMS AND TUBERS

Name	Storage Organ	Hardiness	Description/Cultural Hints	Planting Density
Achimenes	Catkin-like rhizome	Tender	Grow the named hybrids, some of which are ideal for hanging baskets; profusions of flowers in rich colours, late summer and autumn. Erect types need twiggy sticks for support. Likes moderate warmth, humidity, and slight shade.	5 per 130mm pot
Anemone	Small tuber	Hardy	The single-flowered De Caen and the double St Brigid are well known; wide range of glorious colours. Anemone blanda, with daisy-like flowers, can also be grown in pots.	5–7 per 180mm pot
Begonia	Tuber	Tender	Tuberous begonias are an important group. The giant-flowered types are most impressive. Remove the single female flowers, on each side of the large showy male flowers, as early as possible. The pendulous forms, with tassel blooms are wonderful for hanging baskets or pots. Give moderate shade.	Large flowered: 1 per 130mm pot Pendulous: 3 per basket
Bulbocodium vernum	Bulb	Hardy	Corms with crocus-like purplish flowers appearing very early in the year.	5–7 per 180mm pot
Chionodoxa luciliae	Bulb	Hardy	Beautiful blue starry flowers with white centres early in the year. *C. gigantea* has larger flowers. Excellent for a cold conservatory.	5–7 per 180mm pot
Crocus	Bulb	Hardy	These are favourites for pots or bowls in the cold conservatory. Choice named types are available for indoor culture; the extra-large-flowered forms are especially beautiful.	7 per 180mm pot
Cyclamen	Tuber	Tender	The tender cyclamen (not the hardy types) can be potted from July to August for flowering from winter to spring. Many fancy forms.	1 per 130mm pot
Erythronium	Bulb	Hardy	Some species have attractive variegated foliage and pendant starry flowers. Good for shaded positions.	5–7 per 180mm pot
Freesia	Corm	Tender	For best results purchase *named* types recommended for pot culture. Some, but not all, are fragrant. Will flower in winter if potted in summer.	7 per 130mm pot
Galanthus	Bulb	Hardy	This genus includes the well-loved snowdrop; there are also some especially choice large-flowered forms ideally suited to pots or bowls.	Plant generously
Gloriosa	Tuber	Tender	The glory lily. Tuberous climbers. The most frequently grown is *G. rothschildiana*, which has flowers like reflexed lilies, borne summer to autumn. Plant the tubers with the thick end just under the compost surface and the thin end protruding. Slightly poisonous: handle carefully.	1 per 180mm pot
Gloxinia	Corm	Tender	Clusters of huge trumpet flowers in rich colours and velvety green foliage. Flowers summer to autumn. The named hybrids are especially showy.	1 per 130mm pot

COLOURFUL BULBS, CORMS AND TUBERS

Name	Storage Organ	Hardiness	Description/Cultural Hints	Planting Density
Haemanthus	Bulb	Tender	The blood lily. One of the most spectacular species is *H. multiflorus*, which has enormous spherical, crimson flowers, shaped like dandelion clocks. It is grown like hippeastrum.	1 per 120mm pot
Hippeastrum	Bulb	Tender	Bears enormous trumpet flowers in various fine colours on a thick stalk. Foliage often comes after flowers in newly potted bulbs. Pot with the tip well above the compost surface. Do not dry off over winter – the bulb is *evergreen*. Often sold erroneously as amaryllis.	1 per 180mm pot
Hyacinth	Bulb	Hardy	One of the best-known pot plants. There are very many named cultivars and wide range of colours.	1 per 130mm pot 3 per 180mm pot
Lachenalia	Bulb	Tender	*Lachenalia bulbifera* (*L. pendula*) is beautiful in hanging baskets in the conservatory. *L. aloides* 'Nelsonii' has a more erect habit and is better for pots. The flowers are tubular, in shades of yellow and red. Bulbs are best potted during August for flowering about December. Keep cool but frost free.	5–7 per 130mm pot 14cm apart in hanging baskets
Lilium	Bulb	Hardy	Lilies make delightful conservatory plants and there are many kinds suited to pots. Bulbs can be obtained that flower from summer to autumn. Low-growing lilies, such as forms of *L. umbellatum*, are best for pots.	1 per 180mm pot
Muscari	Bulb	Hardy	Grape Hyacinth. Looks well grown in pots. White forms as well as blue are available, some are fragrant. The form *M. comosum plumosum* has flowers forming clusters of bluish filaments.	5 per 130mm pot
Narcissus	Bulb	Hardy	This group includes the daffodil. Dwarf species are charming for pots and bowls and are seen at their best with weather protection, as are double-flowered narcissi. The group is invaluable for cold conservatories.	5 per 180mm pot 8 per 250mm pot
Nerine	Bulb	Tender	Bears umbels of flowers, often with unusual colours and a glistening sheen. Pot in *August* for flowering autumn to early winter. Grow *only* the named varieties developed for pots.	1 per 130mm pot
Tulip	Bulb	Hardy	Choose carefully, not all do well in pots. Best are the early doubles which are short stemmed and strong with showy flowers. Some of the early singles are also good. 'Brilliant Star' is a favourite crimson red variety.	5 per 180mm pot 8 per 150mm pot
Vallota	Bulb	Tender	Scarborough lily. *V. speciosa* is usually grown. It should be treated like hippeastrum. A fine conservatory plant, with large scarlet trumpet flowers in autumn. Pot in August.	1 per 150mm pot

Hippeastrum

Lachenalia

Grape hyacinth

USEFUL FLOWERING PLANTS

Many pot plants can be bought from florist shops and large stores. Garden centres are another source. Those plants described as 'houseplants' are often excellent for the greenhouse and conservatory, frequently growing more vigorously there than in the house itself, which rarely provides a good environment for flowering plants. Most of these plants have been grown by rooting cuttings. You can often increase your stock in the same way once you have established them (see page 52).

Above *Azalea, variety 'Addy Wery', is an evergreen, which has glossy leaves and masses of glorious coral-red flowers.*

AZALEA (Rhododendron).

There are two kinds, one hardy and the other tender. The easiest to grow and also the best for greenhouses or conservatories are the hardy evergreen named types, often sold by nurseries and garden centres. Those sold by florists around Christmas are Indian azaleas (*Rhododendron simsii*) which are specially forced. They will not flower again at the same time of year if kept and must be overwintered in a greenhouse. During summer, azaleas can be stood outdoors in a shady place, but watering must not be forgotten. When potting, use an acid, ericaceous compost and, if possible, water with *clean* rainwater.

BELOPERONE

Shrimp plant is the name given to *B. guttata* because of the strange colour and appearance of the bracts around the flowers. When buying for the greenhouse, it is wise to remove the flowers and bracts that have already formed. This encourages the plant to grow larger and become more decorative. Shade is often recommended, but good light, even some direct sunlight, produces superior colouring. A minimum winter temperature of about 7°C (45°F) is needed.

CAMELLIA

It is not widely realized that these well-known evergreens make fine pot plants when young, and flower well. They make superb conservatory plants, especially where conditions tend to be chilly. With glass protection, blooming is early and the flowers are not ruined by weather as so often happens outdoors. Give an acid, ericaceous compost and water with *clean* rainwater if possible. Do not allow the pots to dry out at any time. This needs to be watched particularly if the plants are stood out for the summer.

CAMPANULA

C. isophylla is an old favourite for hanging baskets in conservatories. It forms an attractive cascade and becomes smothered with blue or white flowers from about July to Autumn. Sometimes leaf variegation occurs spontaneously. When this happens the shoot can be removed as a cutting and rooted. Cream and green variegated plants often have smaller flowers.

Below *Italian bellflower,* Campanula isophylla, *is one of the best summer-flowering, trailing plants.*

Glorious chrysanthemum blooms such as these last for several weeks.

CARNATIONS

With a little care you can grow exquisite carnations just like those sold by florists. These are called perpetual flowering (PF for short) because they continue to produce blooms for cutting almost the whole year round. A minimum winter temperature of about 7–10°C (45–50°F) is essential. Provided you have a greenhouse with plenty of light, they usually fit in well with other plants.

Buy named varieties of rooted cuttings from a specialist nursery in early spring. Not all are fragrant. For beginners the 'Sim' varieties are recommended. In recent years low-growing types have been introduced.

Grow the cuttings for a few weeks in small pots and then transfer to 180mm (7in) pots. Usually, young plants have already been 'stopped' by the nurseryman, if not, you should pinch out the tips. Also 'stop' the side shoots that form later, 'stopping' the fastest growing first. Do not 'stop' them all at once. This procedure is to encourage the growth of stems, all of which will bear one large bloom. The small buds that form from the stem or around the main bud (crown bud), must be removed carefully by bending them back. They usually snap off. This is to direct the plant's energy into development of the crown bud.

Special carnation feeds are sold, but a tomato feed will also give good results. The stems need careful support with canes or special wire carnation supports. It is inadvisable to keep plants for more than three years. Calyx splitting, which causes petals to bulge in one place and spoils the bloom, is a common problem. Avoiding wide temperature fluctuations and erratic watering and feeding will help prevent it.

CHRYSANTHEMUMS

These make wonderful conservatory plants. Certain types are also grown for cutting and can follow a tomato crop. When choosing, consult a descriptive catalogue from a specialist nursery since there are so many types. The catalogue will also give guidance regarding 'stopping' which is particularly important for the large-flowered types.

The large-flowered forms are classified according to flower character, for example, 'incurved' when petals turn inwards, and 'reflexed' when they turn outwards. The plants are grown from rooted cuttings. These can be bought in spring and put outdoors in large pots for the summer. They must be carefully staked to prevent wind damage. They need regular watering and feeding and should be 'stopped' at the recommended time. To obtain high quality blooms, allow only a few stems with one bud on each to develop. The large-flowered varieties also need disbudding to ensure the development of one huge bloom on each stem. Transfer the plants to the greenhouse in autumn for the final training and blooming.

Much easier are the Charm types which can be grown from seed. The rooted cuttings or seedlings must be 'stopped' but they can then be allowed to develop naturally. They first form a neat compact bush, then spread out, later becoming smothered with small 'daisy' blooms forming cushions of colour.

Some other chrysanthemums are also easy to grow from seed, notably the F1 and F2 hybrids. For example, 'Autumn Glory' and 'Petit Point' which are neat and compact. Korean hybrids are worth growing too.

CITRUS
Oranges, lemons, limes, grapefruits, and the like are often grown from 'pips'. The results can be disappointing and it is far better to buy named plant varieties or species from a specialist nursery. *Citrus mitis*, which is often sold as a houseplant, is very popular. It has fragrant, white, waxy star-shaped flowers, followed by small oranges the size of a walnut, which remain decorative for most of the year. Pot on when necessary into an acid, ericaceous compost and use *clean* rainwater if your tap water is 'hard'. It likes full sun and can be put outdoors in summer. A minimum winter temperature of 10°C (50°F) is necessary.

CLIVIA MINIATA
This is an impressive conservatory plant with strap-shaped foliage and enormous umbels of large orange flowers in spring. It need only be kept just frost free, but is severely damaged or killed if temperatures fall below freezing. It should be grown in large pots or small tubs and should be left undisturbed until it is seriously root bound. Avoid direct sun and in winter put in an unheated room and water sparingly.

Broom, Cytisus × racemosus, *has arching sprays of fragrant yellow flowers from winter to late spring.*

CYTISUS (brooms)
Two brooms are often sold as houseplants, genista (*C. canariensis*) and *C.* × *racemosus*. If given large pots they will grow to the height of a man. Restricting pot size and severe pruning can keep them more manageable. Genista has scented yellow flowers, spring to summer, and is evergreen. *C.* × *racemosus* has showy, yellow, scented flowers, winter to spring, and greyish-green foliage. Prune back after flowering and stand outdoors for the summer. Do not allow it to dry out at any time; give slight shade. Bring indoors in September and keep cool but frost free. Water liberally during flowering.

ERICA (bell heathers, or heaths)
From about Christmas time onwards, *Erica gracilis*, which has pink or white flowers and *E. hyemalis*, with pink tubular flowers, are sold by florists. These plants are usually forced for early bloom. After flowering, pot into an acid, ericaceous compost and stand outdoors during summer. Do not allow to dry out. Water with clean rainwater if necessary. Return to the greenhouse for winter. A minimum temperature about 7°C (45°F) is needed.

Fuchsia, variety 'Cascade', is one of very many named varieties of this popular pot plant.

FUCHSIAS
Fuchsias are among the most popular of all pot plants. The flowers have a particular fascination and the plants lend themselves to training in various shapes. There are now innumerable varieties and before making a choice it is best to obtain descriptive catalogues from specialist nurseries. The most convenient way to acquire plants is to buy rooted cuttings in spring, which will flower well the first year.

Training is done by pinching out the tips of shoots. This technique, known as 'stopping', causes several new shoots to grow, all of which will carry flowers in due course. It is important to remember to cease 'stopping' about eight weeks before you want the flowers. Some fuchsias are marvellous displayed in hanging baskets.

To train a standard, select a strong-rooted cutting. Do not 'stop' the tip of the cutting, but allow it to grow normally. Do pinch out *all* side shoots that may form, but not leaves growing from the stem. When the stem has reached the desired height, pinch out the tip. This causes many shoots to form below and these should be 'stopped' in turn, to produce a bushy 'head'. Leaves can then be removed from the supporting stem. A stout cane will be needed for support.

Fuchsias can be overwintered as long as they are kept frost free, but standards need warmer conditions to prevent die back. Shade them in summer and water well. Give good light in winter and water sparingly.

HYDRANGEA
This is a popular gift plant. After flowering cut off the heads and any straggly growth. Stand outdoors in a shady place with pots plunged. New shoots should form. Cut out the old stems (that produced flowers) just above the new ones. The new shoots should flower the following year. Water with clean rainwater if your tap water is 'hard'. Return to the greenhouse in autumn, but do not allow the temperature to rise much above 10°C (50°F) until February as this could inhibit flowering. The flowers will not have rich colour if the compost is alkaline. Use an acid, ericaceous compost for potting.

NERIUM (Oleander)
An ideal evergreen plant for the cool conservatory. Masses of flowers are produced from summer to autumn, in white, pink, and shades of carmine. The plants become untidy unless properly pruned. Shoots that form at the base of the flower trusses should be removed promptly, and in autumn, after flowering, the shoots of the previous year's development should be reduced to about a finger's length. This will encourage new growth from the base. Water well in summer and sparingly in winter. Keep frost free. Note that the sap is poisonous so handle with great care. It can be kept in 200mm (8in) pots for some years.

Hydrangeas last in flower for a very long time if kept cool, moist and shaded.

Oleander, Nerium oleander, *bears pretty, fragrant flowers in clusters above willow-like foliage.*

ORCHIDS

The great majority of orchids we cultivate are hybrids created by man. There are many that grow well alongside other plants in our greenhouses and conservatories – it is not essential to have special conditions. Some people think that orchids are difficult and expensive. This is just not true; they can be cheaper and easier than some other plants we grow.

Orchids do need a special compost of fibrous texture, but this is easy enough to obtain from nurseries specializing in the plants. Such nurseries are also the best source for the orchids themselves. Try to visit nurseries and choose your plants when most orchids are in flower, from winter to spring. Some large stores now also sell fine plants. Since the average home greenhouse or conservatory has a cool winter minimum, it's wise to select orchids accordingly. Undoubtedly top of the list should be the cymbidiums. These bear arching stems of typical orchid flowers with delightful colours and markings, and the blooms are amazingly long lasting. They do very well in a 'mixed' greenhouse. During summer they can be put in a bright position outside.

Many people find paphiopedilums fascinating because of their slipper shape and quaint markings. There are plain-leaved and mottled-leaved kinds; the former are usually better for cool conditions. Unlike most, these orchids do not have pseudobulbs, and they need more shade than cymbidiums. Cattleyas are very exotic and need a higher temperature, but they are compact, and perhaps just part of the greenhouse could be specially heated for them. You could also consider growing the beautiful odontoglossums, miltonias (pansy orchids), and some laelias and vandas.

Orchid growers will advise you on which plants are most suitable for the conditions you have. They will also probably have useful literature giving details of the best treatment for all the many, very varied orchid types available.

PELARGONIUMS

These rival fuchsias in popularity. There are a large number of named cultivars and when choosing you should consult a specialist catalogue.

The plant commonly called 'geranium' is, in fact, the **zonal** pelargonium. The named types now have considerable competition from the F1 hybrids which are easily grown from seed. Most of the group have zoned leaf markings. There are many colours, as well as doubles, semi-doubles, types with variously shaped petals and miniatures. Also some with beautiful leaf colouring and variegation.

The **regal** group have exceptionally showy flowers but these are not borne over such a long period. They are best kept in a greenhouse and can reach a considerable size after a few years. They are very impressive when in flower.

The **ivy-leaved** group are long flowering and particularly suitable for hanging-baskets. Use three or four plants per basket.

All these can be bought as rooted cuttings. 'Stopping' is important to prevent lanky, untidy development. Overwinter in the same conditions as fuchsias and be sure to ventilate freely when possible. Most pelargoniums need plenty of light, and moderate ventilation. Do not overwater.

Cymbidium is the best type of orchid for the beginner. It has all the exotic orchid qualities yet it is easy to grow.

Madagascar jasmine, Stephanotis floribunda, *so-called because of the exquisite but heavy scent of its flowers.*

STEPHANOTIS FLORIBUNDA
(Madagascar jasmine)

An evergreen climber with waxy white tubular flowers having a powerful fragrance. Although it will often survive conditions little more than frost free, it really prefers moderate warmth and humidity. In good conditions it will climb up into the roof of a greenhouse. The stems should be trained on a support and cut back after flowering. Water well in summer and sparingly in winter. It likes a position of moderate light.

STRELITZIA REGINA
(Bird-of-paradise flower)

This is one of the most spectacular of all pot plants, the famous bird-of-paradise flower. It has bold, evergreen spear-shaped leaves and large flowers in orange and blue like an exotic bird's head. The flowers, produced twice a year in summer and at Christmas, are on tall stalks and last for several weeks. Although its appearance is exotic it is, in fact ideal for a frost-free conservatory and does not demand high temperatures, as is often stated. Give a position in good light, but shade from hot sun. Water well in summer and very sparingly in winter. A mature plant needs a 250mm (10in) pot or larger, and should be left until seriously pot bound. Large plants that have 'clumped' can be divided by cutting through the roots in spring. The roots should be separated so that each piece has a 'fan' of leaves. A young plant may take up to two years before it flowers.

The Bird-of-Paradise Flower, Strelitzia reginae, *is actually a member of the banana family although, contrary to popular belief, it does not need hot conditions and is easy to grow.*

TIBOUCHINA

The correct botanical name for this is *Tibouchina urvilleana*, but it's usually labelled *T. semidecandra*. It is a favourite conservatory perennial, bearing pansy-shaped violet-coloured flowers summer to autumn. Buy plants as rooted cuttings and pinch out the top and the tips of any laterals that form after potting. Pot in 180mm (7in) pots for flowering and give a cane for support. Water well in summer and sparingly in winter; cut back severely in late winter.

EASILY GROWN FOLIAGE PLANTS

ARAUCARIA HETEROPHYLLA

The Norfolk Island pine makes a splendid plant for a cool conservatory and can be kept in a 250mm (10in) pot for a long time. It has a form rather like a Christmas tree. It prefers slight shade and good ventilation. If the plants become too large or leggy, cut them back and use the cuttings for propagating new stock. Water well in summer and sparingly in winter. Keep frost free.

The Norfolk Island pine, Araucaria heterophylla, *a handsome plant.*

ASPIDISTRA

This plant is sometimes known humorously as the cast-iron plant because of its resistance to neglect. When looked after well, it can be quite handsome. The cream variegated form should be especially looked for. The plants do well in slight shade and their appearance can be greatly enhanced by treatment with a leaf-shine product. A minimum temperature of 7°C (45°F) is needed.

BEGONIA

There are many extremely beautiful foliage begonias. Most are liable to deteriorate at temperatures below about 10°C (50°F), and they like slight shade and moderate humidity in summer. *Begonia rex* is a favourite, with exotically marked and coloured leaves often splashed silver. The iron cross begonia (*B. masoniana*), so named because of the bold cross mark on its leaves, is also most attractive. Many begonias bear flowers as well as striking foliage, but only rarely can the flowers compete in catching the eye, as in *B. corallina* and *B. tiger*, for example.

BROMELIADS

This group of plants belongs to the pineapple family and is found in nature growing in moss or leaf debris, often above ground in tree branches or rocks. This indicates how they should be grown, that is, in a mossy, leafy compost. There are many bromeliads to choose from. A number produce exotic 'flowers' which are mostly composed of coloured bracts. The species with the more striking leaves may have the least interesting flowers. Most plants form a rosette of foliage with a central 'cup', called an 'urn'. Keep this topped up with water, otherwise water or spray sparingly from the top of the plant only. Most will survive a minimum temperature of about 10°C (50°F).

CALADIUM
This delightful plant is best bought in the form of a large tuber which can be started into growth in spring, in a warm propagator. Large handsome arrow-shaped leaves, veined and marked with various lovely colours, are soon produced. It loves warmth and humidity but is easily grown from tubers. When the foliage fades, let the pots become almost dry. Then store indoors over winter at a minimum temperature of 13°C (55°F).

CHLOROPHYTUM CAPENSE (spider plant)
This is a very popular and adaptable plant. From a clump of arching foliage grow long stems bearing small white flowers followed by tiny plantlets. It makes a fine basket plant for the conservatory, given about 7°C (45°F) minimum temperature in winter.

CISSUS ANTARCTICA
This is a climber which, in greenhouse conditions, can reach the roof. It has pale green, spear-shaped leaves with toothed edges. Despite the name it needs a winter minimum of about 5°C (41°F). Watch out for aphid attack and red spider to which the plant is prone. Give an 180mm (7in) pot with good drainage. To encourage bushy growth pinch out the stem tips.

Blue Gum, Eucalyptus globulus, *has very attractive grey-blue-green juvenile foliage.*

EUCALYPTUS
Many species make fine foliage plants for the cool conservatory, but they can become very large. The blue gum (*Eucalyptus globulus*) is popular and is easy to grow from seed. Look out also for the dwarf golden gum (*E. exima nana*), the silver gum (*E. cordata*) and the alpine gum (*E. archeri*). Eucalypts have attractive juvenile leaves, which may be lost on maturity. Fortunately, new plants are usually easy to grow from seed. Many species produce the familiar eucalyptus aroma and will scent the greenhouse during periods of warm weather.

EUONYMUS
The attractive dwarf evergreen varieties are excellent foliage plants for cold conditions and deserve to be grown more often in conservatories. Especially recommended are *Euonymus japonica* 'Variegata' and 'Aurea', and *E. fortunei* 'Vegeta' and 'Silver Queen'. The variegated foliage looks its best during winter. They are generally slow growers, but 'Silver Queen' can grow tall if allowed.

Bromeliad, Neoregelia carolinae, *often called the nest plant because of the central cup.*

× *FATSHEDERA*
This bigeneric cross between *Fatsia* and *Hedera* has characteristics of both and is excellent for chilly places. The best form is 'Variegata' which has cream variegated, glossy ivy-like leaves, but needs to be kept frost free. It can be trained as a bush by pruning, or led up supports as a climber. Do not overwater.

FATSIA JAPONICA
Although this can be raised from seed (see page 50) the cream variegated form cannot. This is a desirable form but is not so hardy and is best kept frost free. Its foliage is a glossier, lighter green.

FERNS
There are very many ferns from which to choose, and a good selection is readily obtainable. Some recommended species are ribbon fern (*Pteris cretica*); ladder fern (*Nephrolepis exaltata*); holly fern (*Cyrtomium falcatum*), which has an unusual appearance; bird's nest fern (*Asplenium nidus*); and *Polypodium vulgare* in its choice forms. Most of the hardy garden ferns can be grown in pots but it's preferable to choose evergreen subjects. They usually do well in shaded places and are ideal in north-facing conservatories or under the staging.

Below *Bird's Nest Fern,* Asplenium nidus, *has large fronds with wavy edges and dark midribs.*

FICUS
The best-known species is the rubber plant (*Ficus elastica*). This, however, needs a minimum temperature of 10°C (50°F) to remain decorative. Relatively hardy and ideal for chilly conservatories are the mistletoe fig (*F. deltoidea*), which bears reddish to yellow berries all year round, and the creeping fig (*F. pumila*) which is a trailer but can also be grown up supports. In both, the foliage is small and dainty.

Above *The Canary Island ivy,* Hedera canariensis.

HEDERA (Ivy)
There are many ivies of variable appearance, leaf form and height size. All are useful for cold shady places. One of the most impressive is *Hedera canariensis* which has cream and two-tone-green variegation. This species is hardy, but will grow rampantly in warmth. Sudden wide temperature changes may, however, lead to leaf shedding. It will reach roof height if allowed.

MONSTERA DELICIOSA (Swiss cheese plant)
This well-known houseplant has leaves which are perforated when mature and lobed when young. It can grow to well over a man's height in good conditions and is happy in surprisingly small pots. It sends down long aerial roots to enter the compost and can survive almost freezing temperatures. If kept at above 13°C (55°F), it may produce arum-like flowers and elongate pineapple-like fruits.

Right *The Swiss Cheese plant,* Monstera deliciosa, *can grow very tall. Use a moss-covered stake for support and for moisture for aerial roots.*

Chamaerops humilis *is a stately fan palm which makes an ideal specimen plant.*

PALMS

There are a number of hardy palms for gardens that can be grown in pots indoors and are ideal for chilly conservatories. For example, *Chamaerops humilis* and *Phoenix canariensis*, which is almost hardy. Several are sold as houseplants and grow very well in cool greenhouses or conservatories. The *Howeia* palms are especially good, but need 7°C (45°F) winter minimum. Palms seem to grow well in comparatively small pots. Water well in summer and sparingly in winter. Pot-on every two years at the most when young.

PELARGONIUM (Scented geranium)

This group of pelargoniums is noted for leaf fragrance and few have much in the way of showy flowers. They are named according to their scent. For example, nutmeg, lemon, orange, rose bowl, and peppermint. They can be grown much like other pelargoniums, in general, and have the same preferences for light and air. They are most desirable in conservatories, where they often scent the air when conditions are warm. Specialist pelargonium nurseries will have a good selection from which to choose.

Aluminium plant, Pilea cadieri, *is grown for the beauty of its silvery leaves.*

PILEA CADIEREI (aluminium plant)

There are a number of pileas, but this species is the most common and is easy to grow. Its attractive silvery foliage suggests its common name. It is neat and bushy in habit and is useful where space is limited. It can suffer from magnesium deficiency, causing leaf distortion and poor growth. Treat by adding a few crystals of Epsom salts from time to time.

SAXIFRAGA STOLONIFERA (mother of thousands)

This well-known pot plant has long runners carrying baby plants which can be detached and rooted. Look out for the superior variety 'Tricolor', which has roundish pinkish veined leaves. It is slower growing but very attractive. Keep frost free. It is very useful for wall pots, shelves and similar positions.

SOLEIROLIA SOLEIROLII (mind your own business)

So-called because of its creeping invasive habit, this plant is mat forming and therefore very useful for creating 'carpet' effects; it will grow over the surface of beds and pots to hide them and produce a natural effect. Do not allow it to dry out at any time. Winter at 5–7°C (41–45°F).

TOLMIEA MENZIESII (pick-a-back plant)

This plant is so called because of the little plantlets that form around the leaf edges. These can be detached and easily rooted. A creeping plant with prettily marked foliage. It produces spikes of pinky flowers in summer and is useful for shelves, hanging containers, edges of staging and similar positions; ideal for chilly conditions. There is a variegated form but it is not so hardy.

TRADESCANTIA

Tradescantia fluminensis, in its various forms, is a popular trailing houseplant. Its pretty markings and colours develop best if it is given good light and not overwatered. It is frequently confused with *Zebrina pendula*, which has leaves that are green and silver above, and purplish below. This plant does tolerate shade and will often grow under staging. Keep well pruned and propagate from cuttings.

Mother of Thousands, Saxifraga stolonifera. *The runners bearing the baby plants can be left to hang freely and the plant be displayed in a hanging basket or over the edge of a shelf.*

CACTI AND OTHER SUCCULENTS

There is a vast range of these attractive plants, and many can be grown successfully in a mixed greenhouse collection. With few exceptions they need a lot of light and make a good choice for such places as a south-facing conservatory. They can survive without water for quite a time and, therefore, are ideal if you are unable to give regular care. This obviously does not mean that they can be left without water indefinitely. During summer most need plenty of water but they should be left to rest on the dry side in winter. Many produce quite showy flowers. Make your choice from the following selection.

Peanut cactus, Chamaecereus silvestrii, *is easy to grow and can flower profusely.*

Left *Thread agave,* Agave filifera, *is a succulent, with thread-like filaments on its spiky leaves.*

CACTI AND SUCCULENTS

Plant	Category	Description
Agave	Succulent	Rosettes of long sword-like leaves, sometimes with cream striping.
Aloe	Succulent	Many have rosettes of spiny, attractively marked leaves and spikes of flowers.
Cephalocereus senilis	Cactus	Old man cactus. Cylindrical in appearance with dense coating of long grey hair.
Chamaecereus silvestrii	Cactus	Peanut cactus. Forms a mat of finger-like stems and produces brilliant scarlet, starry flowers.
Cotyledon	Succulent	Shrubby plants with attractively coloured foliage. Most have pendulous flowers.
Crassula	Succulent	A large group of variable shape and appearance, mostly very easy to grow. *C. argentia* is known as the jade plant.
Echinocactus grusonii	Cactus	A popular species with globular form, and spines, Slow growing, eventually becoming large.
Echinocereus	Cactus	Ribbed, free flowering and easy to grow.
Epiphyllums	Cactus	A group containing many named hybrids with enormous flowers, freely produced.
Euphorbia obesa	Succulent	Often called Turkish temple because of shape. Slow grower, eventually reaching the size of an orange. *E. milii* is also popular.
Kalanchoe	Succulent	Flaming Katy. Large range of hybrids, popularly grown from seed.
Lithops	Succulent	So-called living stones because of their pebble-like appearance. They have very showy flowers.
Mammillaria	Cactus	Globular in shape and spiny; encircled with delightful flowers.
Schlumbergera	Cactus	A popular group that includes the Christmas cactus, crab cactus and Easter cactus. All have attractive flowers.

FRUIT AND VEGETABLES

Growing food crops in the greenhouse can be very worthwhile financially. There are also other important benefits. You can be sure of a fresh supply that has excellent flavour and texture, is high in vitamins and conveniently at hand at any time. Useful food crops can be grown all year round and, with careful planning, you can usually fit them in with most of your favourite decorative plants, thus getting the best of both worlds.

For home greenhouse gardeners it is important, as we have already seen, to avoid using the ground soil for growing. You can grow most food crops in containers of some kind. Proprietary growing bags and growing boards, which swell up after the addition of water and are easier to transport, are very popular now. Since some crops need quite a large quantity of compost, DIY mixes of peat and grit, with added proprietary, premixed balanced fertilizers, can be made up for economy.

Most food crops require good light conditions. In gloom they may crop badly and have poor quality and flavour. Glass-to-ground greenhouses and those sited in open, light positions, usually give best results, especially for winter crops.

Even the most efficiently run greenhouses are liable to invasion by pests and diseases. If you use pesticides on food crops, make a special point of reading the labels carefully. Some are safer than others; some are too toxic and not suitable at all. The edible safety period for harvesting after treatment must be noted and followed exactly.

Most of the edible crops are cheaply raised from seed. The sowing technique is much the same as that for decorative plants (see page 50).

Electric soil-warming cables can be extremely useful in growing some crops. They are invaluable for warming frames in the greenhouse and for gently forcing winter and early salad crops. They can also be used to provide a little extra root warmth for various other crops so that you can enjoy them earlier.

AUBERGINE

This is grown in much the same way as the sweet pepper (see page 45), but it needs a strong cane to support the heavy fruits. Allow only two or three fruits to mature per plant; pick the others off as early as possible. The young plants can be 'stopped' to encourage short bushy growth but this delays cropping. The plants can grow to about 1m (3ft) without 'stopping'. Grow them in large pots or growing bags. The variety 'Early Purple' can be recommended. It is best to pick the ripe aubergines while the 'bloom' or shine is still on them because when this goes they begin to have a bitter flavour.

CABBAGE AND CAULIFLOWER

The cabbage varieties 'Hispi' and 'May Star' can be sown January/March for planting out later and harvesting from May onwards. Transfer seedlings, initially, to small pots for growing on. In very cold areas, autumn sow and plant out in early March.

Cauliflowers for starting under glass must be chosen carefully from those varieties sold for sowing in September and harvesting May/June. Winter cauliflower (curding broccoli) can be sown April/May for cropping January. There are both hardy and less hardy varieties. Select according to your greenhouse temperature. Keep plants in frames during the summer. When moved to the greenhouse, space them 450mm (18in) apart.

CAPE GOOSEBERRY

This plant is related to the garden ornamental Chinese lantern. In the greenhouse it is cultivated for the golden-yellow berries that develop inside the lantern-shaped husks. The berries are about the size of large cherries and golden yellow when ready to eat. They have a pleasant, refreshing flavour eaten raw and can also be cooked and used in preserves.

For greenhouse culture choose the variety 'Golden Berry'. Grow the plants at first in the same way as tomatoes (see page 46). Use the same size pots and place in a light position. The height to which they are grown can vary considerably. You can 'stop' the plants at an early stage to encourage bushy growth and to get more fruits, but avoid too much 'stopping' since it may delay fruiting. The main harvest should be about late summer.

The true Cape gooseberry is *Physalis peruviana* (*P. edulis*) but, as grown, other species may be involved.

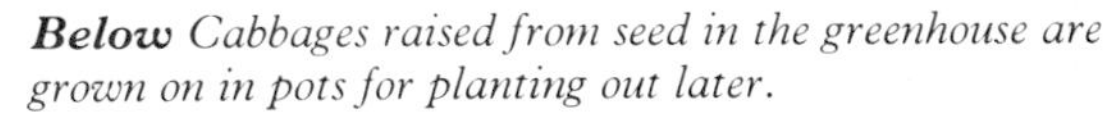
Below *Cabbages raised from seed in the greenhouse are grown on in pots for planting out later.*

Above *French beans should be picked young. The pods should snap off the plant.*

CLIMBING FRENCH BEAN

The ideal minimum temperature for this crop is about 13°C (55°F) – it's wise not to start it too early in the year. Late winter is probably the best time. Grow the plants in the same way as tomatoes (see page 46) and in the same position, spacing 350mm (14in) apart. Provide strings for the plants to climb up, and 'stop' the laterals and secondary laterals (side shoots) at the third joint. A recent new variety recommended for the greenhouse is 'Selka'. The crop should be mature by late spring. Gather at once for best flavour and clear the site which can then be used for tomatoes.

Training and 'stopping' are essential for a good crop of high quality cucumbers.

CUCUMBER

The home-grown cucumber can far excel the shop-bought product. The flavour, crispness, and digestibility of modern varieties are excellent and, nowadays, they are easy to grow; there are all-female varieties needing little attention to prevent pollination (see below), there are new pesticides available that do not harm the cucumber family in general. The crop can be grown alongside other plants including tomato. There is also often greater tolerance of low temperatures.

Ordinary varieties bear both male and female flowers and it is vital to prevent pollination of the females. Do this by promptly picking off the male flowers, which are the ones without tiny fruits attached. If pollination occurs, the fruits will go to seed, becoming club-shaped and sometimes bitter in taste. The 'all-female' varieties produce few, if any, male flowers and, although the seed is more expensive, the yield and flavour is usually far superior.

Sow the flattish seeds on their sides in small pots. Early March is a good sowing time. Germination occurs in a few days at about 18°C (64°F). Grow on in small pots in the same way as tomatoes (see page 46), subsequently planting into large pots or growing bags. If you want only a few fruits, the plants can be trained up canes. Training properly on strings should ensure cropping over a long period.

For proper training it is best to set the growing containers at staging level. The roof above should be fitted with strings running lengthways about 200mm (8in) apart. At first, grow the plants as a single stem up the greenhouse side with canes for support. Remove all side shoots. When a plant reaches the roof, lead it under the strings. Laterals which then form should be led along the nearest string. By the time four leaves have formed, the female flowers should also have developed. Now 'stop' the shoot. Secondary laterals will now grow out and can be secured to a string and treated in a similar manner. The main stem should be 'stopped' when it has reached the uppermost string.

Keep the compost moist, but be very careful not to overwater. Wet conditions quickly cause deterioration, leaves go yellow and fruits start to rot, or drop while immature. The best quality is obtained when plants are grown so that the fruits form and mature quickly.

FIG

Given a free root run, figs can become far too rampant and invasive for the home greenhouse, so it's wise to grow them in large free-standing pots or small tubs. This way the plants can be put outdoors in summer, which saves space and seems to improve the crop. However, some people do prefer to fan-train them against the wall of a lean-to, which should preferably be south facing. The most popular variety is 'Brown Turkey'. This is available, container grown, from garden centres.

The best planting time is spring. When the fruit is borne, 'stop' the fruit-bearing shoots about four leaves beyond, and allow only about three or four fruits per shoot to develop. The fruits are upright as they develop. When they hang down they are ripe and can be picked. Prune in spring, cutting out weak or excessive growth.

The fig 'Brown turkey' has medium-sized fruit.

A grape vine should bear a good crop like this by its third year.

GRAPE

The grape vine is not a good companion for other plants. It does not want heat in winter and it can also severely cut out the light level. The best management can be given when the plant has a house to itself. Lean-tos make particularly good vineries.

The traditional way to grow the vines is to plant the roots outside the greenhouse, in a border running alongside. The stems, called 'rods', are then led through small holes made along the base and up inside the greenhouse. The roots can be put inside the greenhouse, but various troubles due to drying out and soil sickness are then liable to develop. Plant early in the year and then cut back the roots to about 450mm (18in). For the average greenhouse, allow two shoots to grow, leading them horizontally in opposite directions. The lateral shoots that grow from these can be trained vertically. Shoots from this upright growth should be stopped when 600mm (2ft) long, and cut back in winter. The main upright shoots should then be cut back too.

The side shoots must be fastened to wires in the second year and all laterals reduced to one or two buds in winter. A few bunches of grapes may appear in the second year, and the third year should bring a good crop. However, do not allow more than one bunch to form on each lateral. The bunches must be thinned. Do this with finely tipped scissors, without touching the grapes with your fingers as this spoils the 'bloom'.

No heating is necessary in winter but during flowering try to maintain a minimum temperature of 13°C (55°F). Efficient ventilation is essential to deter mildew, which is a common problem.

Although vines are now container grown and sold by garden centres, it's advisable to buy from a specialist grower who will also suggest suitable varieties.

Grape vines can be grown in pots. 'Royal Muscadine' and 'Black Hamburgh' have long been cultivated in this way. The vines are potted at Christmas and put outdoors at first. In late winter they are taken into the greenhouse where no heating is necessary. They are trained on a pair of vertical bamboos, up one and then down the other. Laterals must be thinned to about 300mm (12in) apart and 'stopped' two leaves from where a bunch of grapes develops. You receive only about six bunches per plant and the plants have to be discarded after three years.

Kiwi fruit grow only on a female plant but a male one is essential for pollination.

KIWI FRUIT

Also known as the Chinese gooseberry, this is becoming more widely available in fruit shops. It is a brownish, furry, elongate fruit about the size of a large egg, and is quite delicious. *Actinidia chinensis* makes a good wall shrub for a lean-to greenhouse or conservatory. Buy the plants from a specialist nursery in pairs – a male and a female. The former is needed for pollination and can be planted outside the greenhouse provided it's close by. Insects will then usually visit both plants, but to be sure of fruit, you can hand pollinate the creamy-yellow female flowers using fluffed-up cotton wool. Plants can also be grown in large pots. 'Stop' them when young to produce branching for wall training. Prune in February.

LETTUCE

This crop can be grown in the greenhouse for gathering from winter to spring. It is essential to choose suitable varieties (see below) since some are quite unsatisfactory for cultivation under glass.

Lettuce can be grown in troughs or trenches of specially prepared compost or in pots. Some people use ground soil but the crop is often then attacked by grey mould, which causes the plant to wilt or collapse.

Sow the seed as described on page 50. Prick out the seedlings into seed trays for growing-on and transfer them to permanent positions when large enough to handle. Give good light and ventilation.

The variety 'Kwiek' is suitable for a cold greenhouse, and should be sown in late summer to crop in winter. 'Kloek' can also be grown in cold conditions but should be sown in autumn for spring use. 'Sea Queen', which can be grown in either cool or cold conditions, is sown in late summer or winter for winter or spring cropping. 'Emerald' can be treated similarly. Sow 'May Queen' in autumn or spring in a cold or cool greenhouse for spring or summer cropping. 'Dandie', which is a fast maturing variety, can be sown in autumn to give you a good crop from late autumn onwards.

A bumper crop of greenhouse-grown lettuces.

'Early Sweet' is a large Cantaloupe melon, which can be grown like the Casaba type.

MELON

The best melons to grow in the greenhouse are the very large Casaba types. The small kinds, such as Musk or Cantaloupe, are more suitable for frame culture.

Treatment is the same as for cucumber in the early stages. The training is also similar, but differs in that the strings for support, which must be strong, should be spaced further apart, about 300mm (12in). The female flowers must be deliberately pollinated. Do this by removing a male flower, which is one with no swelling behind it on the stalk, and transferring the pollen directly to the female flowers, which have the swelling. Successful pollination is indicated by the swellings becoming larger and soon taking the form of tiny melons.

Melons need plenty of light and there is rarely need for shading. Allow only three to four fruits on each plant. When the fruit has matured, avoid excessive humidity and ventilate more freely than before. Owing to their weight, the fruit may need supporting with netting; you can improvise with string bags. Fruit is ripe when the opposite end from the stalk feels soft when you press it with a finger; and when it gives off a fruity aroma.

Recommended varieties are 'Superlative', 'Hero of Lockinge', and 'Emerald Gem'. The Cantaloupe melon, 'Early Sweet', is a vigorous F1 hybrid and larger than others of this kind. It can be grown like the Casabas. Of the Cantaloupes the variety 'No Name' is especially recommended for unheated frames. Sow and raise initially in the greenhouse.

MUSHROOM

The mushroom is the fungus *Psalliota campestris*. It is a useful crop for the understage area, if a temperature of about 10°C (50°F) minimum can be maintained. The area can be sectioned off and heated with soil warming cables for economy, if desired. Mushroom growing is normally an elaborate procedure requiring special composts and spawn. However, it is now made easy by the availability of ready-spawned 'buckets' stocked by most seedsmen. Full instructions, which are quite simple, are provided. You can obtain a constant supply of fresh, delicious mushrooms using this method, but they may not be cheap.

PEACH, NECTARINE, APRICOT

These, like the grape, are not generally suitable for growing in a mixed greenhouse collection. The ideal site for them is the rear wall of a south-facing lean-to. They are grown in much the same way as other wall-trained outdoor plants, except that hand pollination is usually required. This is simply done by brushing over the flowers lightly with a piece of fluffed-up cotton wool. Midday is the best time to do it.

If you grow them in the greenhouse, keep the atmosphere moderately humid by damping down, but do not spray the flowers with water. Apricots can be tricky and the flowers tend to drop if the temperature rises high and ventilation is inadequate. Contact a specialist nursery when buying the plants. Recently there have been new varieties introduced and also specially dwarfed forms, which are ideal for growing in pots or limited space.

Some old-established varieties are 'Lord Napier' and 'Early Rivers' (nectarine); 'Moorpark' (apricot); 'Hale's Early' and 'Duke of York' (peach).

Mushrooms can be grown easily in bags of ready-spawned compost under greenhouse staging.

SPROUTING SEEDS

Seed sprouts (salad sprouts), which include a variety of plants, have recently received much publicity because of their possible health-giving properties. In particular, they often have high vitamin and protein content and in some cases minerals too. They are delicious, and in winter, salad sprouts can be especially welcome. You can produce an edible crop within about one week.

Many seedsmen offer packets of seeds suitable for sprouting and supply full instructions. The best place to grow them is in a propagator. A temperature of about 20°C (68°F) is desirable, which can be attained in most simple propagating cases. The old favourite, mustard and cress, is included in this group. You can also sprout mung bean (*Phaseolus mungo*) well known because of its use in Chinese cooking, alfalfa (*Medicago sativa*) particularly valuable for winter salads, adzuki beans (*Phaseolus angularis*) with a nutty flavour, and fenugreek (*Trigonella foenum-graecum*).

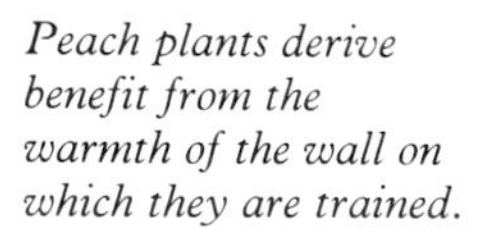

Peach plants derive benefit from the warmth of the wall on which they are trained.

SQUASHES
These include courgettes, marrows, and pumpkins. They are not usually cropped in the greenhouse, but the sowings and initial growing of the young plants can be made under glass to ensure earlier crops. Don't forget to harden off the young plants (see page 51) before putting them outdoors.

Pumpkins, such as this variety, 'Patty Pan', can be started into growth in the greenhouse.

STRAWBERRY
These are really most suited to frames but a few pots can be grown in the greenhouse. They look good planted in special strawberry urns, which are available at most garden centres. Buy the plants freshly each year from a specialist grower who will have the fine modern varieties. Grow them on outdoors until early in the year. Pot up in an approved compost, one plant to each 130mm (5in) pot if desired. The best minimum temperature is 7°C (45°F). Hand pollinate by brushing over the flowers lightly with fluffed-up cotton wool.

Strawberry plants can be decorative as well as useful in a greenhouse.

SWEET PEPPER
The correct common name for this plant is pimiento, but sometimes the incorrect name 'capsicum', suggesting a hot taste, is given. This crop is well worth growing particularly because it is expensive to buy yet quite easy to grow. The F1 hybrid varieties are especially recommended. Initially, treat in the same way as tomatoes (see page 46), sowing the seed at about the same time. Unlike tomatoes, rogueing is not necessary. Pot the young plants finally into 180mm (7in) pots. For some of the taller varieties a cane may be needed for support. From then on little attention, apart from watering, is necessary until the tiny fruits start to form. Depending on variety, you may need to thin these to prevent overcrowding, giving room for those left to develop properly. The fruits are ready to pick from summer onwards. The green fruits ripen through yellow to red, even if picked at the green stage, provided they are stored in a warm place.

Sweet peppers can be picked and eaten when still green or left to ripen to red.

'Big boy' tomato has giant fruits which are firm with good flavour.

TOMATOES

The tomato is the most popular of all home greenhouse crops. Some people fit in a few pots here and there, others give it a large part of the greenhouse. Although the tomato is easy to grow, it can be affected by a variety of problems, but many can be avoided, as they generally arise when the crop is grown in the ground soil for several years. Excellent plants can be grown in large pots, growing bags or other containers. The system of ring culture (see opposite) also works well. The best position for the crop is one with good light. The south side of an east-west greenhouse is ideal.

There are now many seed varieties. 'Moneymaker', is an old favourite but it has been largely replaced by 'Alicante'. Don't be afraid to be adventurous. A selection is given in the table.

Sow the seeds from late winter onwards, using the methods given on page 50. The ideal germination temperature is 16°C (61°F). Prick out the seedlings into 80–100mm (3–4in) pots of an approved potting compost and grow on until well rooted. The plants should then be 'rogued'. This means discarding any that are weak, stunted or distorted, or have pale-coloured or mottled foliage, and any that have a bushy or unusually vigorous habit. Such plants are liable to prove unproductive and may be affected by diseases.

When potting the plants into their final pots, try to use at least 250mm (10in) pots. Fibre disposable pots, usually about 230mm in diameter can also be used. If the pots are too small the roots suffer from erratic changes in water availability and temperature, which should be avoided. Use an approved compost and, when potting, leave a space between the compost surface and the top of the pot. This can be topped up with fresh compost as the plant develops and the compost shrinks.

The plants need strings (use rough string) or canes for support. Train them round these in a clockwise direction. It is essential, as a daily routine, to remove the side shoots that appear at the joints between the main stem and the leaves. To obtain a good set of fruit, distribute the pollen by tapping the plants or spraying with a mist of water when conditions are bright and warm. You can also spray with a hormone setting preparation.

When fruit is ripening, avoid temperatures over 27°C (81°F). With too much heat the red pigment does not form and you may get green rings, or greenish/yellowish blotches. An excellent shading product is found in Coolglass, which gives the right degree of shade for strong growth but does not cast gloom. Remove any foliage that has deteriorated, but avoid excessive defoliation as this weakens plants and can spoil the fruit flavour. Special high potassium tomato feeds are available which should be used according to the label instructions.

When plants reach the greenhouse roof, pinch out the growing tips. This allows the fruit on the plants to reach maturity and ripen before conditions become too cool. It is essential to avoid erratic changes of any kind. Keep the compost moist all the time. Feed often with weak feeds and try to prevent wide temperature fluctuations. If these points are ignored, flower shedding, immature fruit fall, blotchy ripening, split skins, sun scald, or dark-coloured rots at the stalk or flower end of the fruit may occur.

RING CULTURE

This is often used for tomato cultivation but can also be adapted for other similar crops, including aubergine, sweet pepper and cucumber. The plants are grown in bottomless rings. You can buy disposable fibre rings, about 230mm in diameter, made for the purpose. The procedure is as follows. Put down a layer of aggregate, such as clean shingle or, preferably, coarse peat on a strip of polythene to prevent contact with the greenhouse ground soil. The polythene should be slit for drainage here and there if necessary. The rings are then placed on the aggregate, which should be about 130mm (5in) thick, and filled with an approved potting compost, into which the tomatoes are planted. The compost must be kept moist until the roots of the plants have reached the aggregate layer. From then on, water is applied only to the aggregate layer, which is kept constantly moist. Moisture rises up into the compost from the aggregate by capillary action. Feeding with liquid feeds, however, is done via the compost in the rings. The lower roots of the plants are the 'drinking roots' and the upper ones are the 'feeders'. This method gives the plants a highly stable environment and lends itself well to automatic watering systems. It is particularly useful if you have to leave plants unattended for long periods. At the end of the season, discard the aggregate; use fresh material for the next crop to prevent pest and disease carry over.

'Tigerella' is an early tomato with yellow striped fruit.

'Yellow perfection' is a tomato of fine quality and superb flavour.

RECOMMENDED TOMATO VARIETIES

Alicante	Good general quality and disease resistance.
Big boy	Huge fruits of fleshy texture. Excellent for slicing and for sandwiches.
Eurocross A	Similar to Moneymaker, but superior vigour and yield.
Growers pride F1	Recommended for beginners. Good early yield. Generally useful.
Mandel F1	Good disease resistance and generally useful. Dark red colour.
Odine F1	Short jointed and ideal for small greenhouses. Generally useful.
Tigerella	Fruit has yellow stripes. Excellent flavour. Early. Generally useful.
Vibelco	Said to be the most disease resistant of all varieties so far.
Yellow perfection	Golden yellow fruits of exceptional flavour and quality. Must be tried.

PROPAGATION

So that you can make the most of your greenhouse, it is a good idea to become familiar with the techniques used to propagate plants. Once you are proficient in using these you can increase your stock, decrease your expenditure and sometimes help to preserve plants already in your collection. Most forms of propagation are also fascinating and give pleasure in themselves.

Some plants are very easy to propagate, others very difficult. The easy ones tend to become far too numerous, so be wary of accepting all propagating material, such as cuttings, offered by friends. Never use plant material which is itself unhealthy or has been taken from a diseased or pest-infected plant. For propagation, only use the best in both general quality and health. Undesirable characteristics can be inherited as well as desirable ones, and certain diseases, such as virus infections, can also be passed on.

PROPAGATING EQUIPMENT

For the quick and efficient propagation of most greenhouse plants it is best to set aside a specific area. It will need to be warmed from underneath and have a transparent cover to retain heat and moisture while letting in light. You can make up such an area yourself by laying electric warming cables over a part of the staging, covering it with sand, then enclosing it with transparent plastic sheeting or a glass frame. The suppliers of warming cables give recommendations for their use in propagation. As a rough guide, a 120–150 watt cable will heat a space about 1.5m × 600mm (5ft × 2ft). It can be thermostatically controlled. Other forms of electric greenhouse heater, such as tubes (see page 15), can be used, either controlled manually or thermostatically. A paraffin lamp is another possible heat source.

You may prefer to buy a ready-made propagator. These are available with electric or paraffin heaters. Electric ones are preferable, if you have the power supply, because they have a thermostat which makes them easy to control and set for different temperatures as required. For most greenhouse propagation, a range of temperature from little more than frost free, for hardy plants, to about 27°C (80°F), for sub-tropicals, is necessary. Many plants need a high temperature for propagation, higher than they normally require once established, so it's important to check that a propagator can give high temperatures when necessary.

The propagators available vary greatly in size, temperature range, and design. For the greenhouse, choose a covered design that has a variable temperature control and is of a suitable size for your requirements and the amount of space you have available. It is often useful to have room enough to keep plants in congenial warmth after propagation, until they become well established. Large enclosed propagators can be used as a permanent home for a small sub-tropical plant collection.

A mist propagation area, in which propagating material is coated with moisture by a central misting jet and warmed by warming cables.

USING A PROPAGATOR

A propagator should have a base of sand which is always kept moist. The moist sand distributes the warmth evenly and keeps the atmosphere in the propagator humid. Dry conditions must be avoided because propagating material, such as seeds and cuttings, can quickly become dehydrated and die before roots have a chance to form. A transparent cover is also desirable to retain moisture and warmth, particularly for plants needing higher temperatures. Light is another essential for much propagation, but you should avoid direct sunlight. Site the propagator or propagation area where there's slight shade. If necessary, shade an area of the greenhouse glass with white Coolglass. Excessively high temperatures can also cause severe damage, and it is important to remember that the temperature in the propagator is affected by the temperature of its surroundings.

The propagator comes into its own about late winter to spring, when it is used for such purposes as striking cuttings, seed germination, and starting tubers etc. into growth. During the rest of the year there is usually sufficient natural warmth for the types of plants then propagated.

A well-designed, electrically heated, covered propagator. The temperature can be varied and is controlled by a thermostat.

A portable bench or tray provides a conveniently sized hygienic surface for potting and similar tasks.

POTTING BENCH

This is an area of staging set aside for potting, seed sowing, preparation of cuttings, mixing composts and similar operations. A portable bench is a good idea. This can be simply made using a sheet of aluminium or zinc, which is available from most builders' merchants or DIY shops. Select the right size for the chosen section of your staging, then turn up the sides of the sheet to form a three-sided tray to fit the space exactly. Keep the surface clean and wipe down from time to time with disinfectant (see page 55).

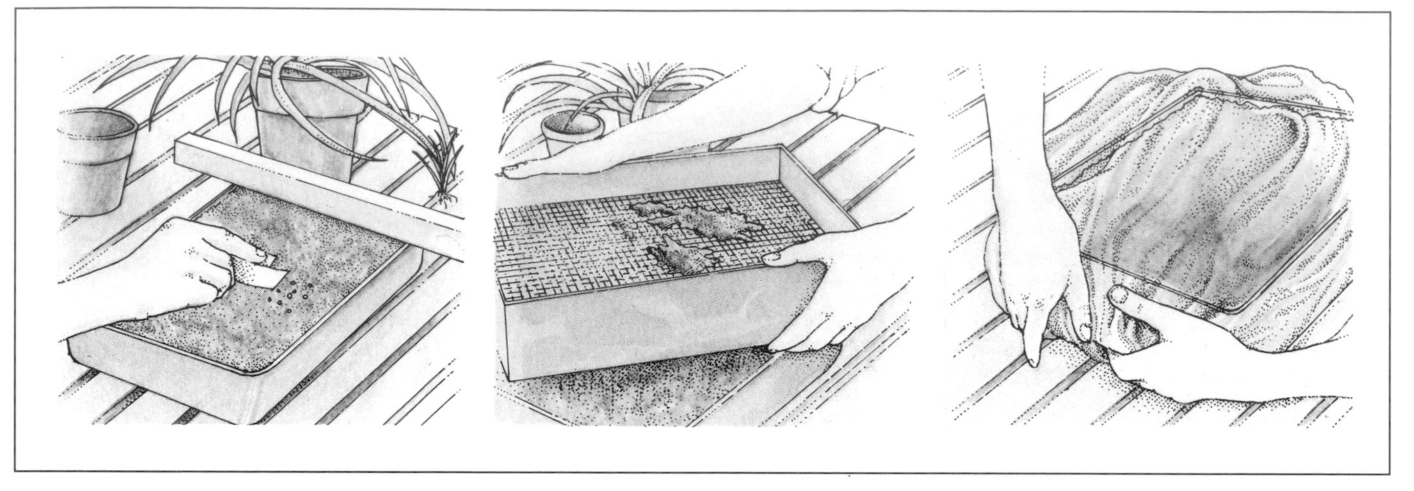

When sowing seed, tap it from the packet with the forefinger. A sieve can be used to riddle compost over very fine seed. Finally, cover the tray with polythene to help retain moisture.

PROPAGATION FROM SEED

Seed is a cheap source of plants and, nowadays, is widely available from plants that grow all over the world.

Sometimes you can save seed from your own plants or from other growing sources. Seed from hybrids, however, particularly F1 hybrids, is usually unreliable. It may not yield plants true to type and should not be saved.

Seed should be ripe and reasonably fresh. Old seed generally germinates poorly. Sow as soon as possible after you get it or, if it has to be kept a while, store in a cool, dry place in the home. Do not leave packets in the damp and heat of a greenhouse. Most seed companies now supply seed in special sealed packs with controlled humidity. Seed will remain viable for a long time when kept in these packs but normal ageing begins once they have been opened.

To make tiny seed easier to handle, some varieties are pelleted with an inert material by the seedsmen. However, there is some difference of opinion about whether this is an advantage, since germination of this type is sometimes poor. To hasten germination, large seeds can be soaked in water overnight before sowing. Another common practice which is used particularly for tough or hard-coated seeds, is to slice off a tiny sliver of the outer coating with a razor blade, being very careful not to damage the interior.

Seed must be sown in proper seed compost to ensure success. You can use John Innes loam-based seed compost or any of the numerous proprietary peat-based seed composts now available. Another essential is general cleanliness. Keep the seed compost in closed plastic bags or containers when not in use. Make sure that the rectangular plastic seed trays in which you put the seed compost are kept clean, as well as the plastic pots which are used for sowing some larger types of seed. Fill the tray or pot by lightly pressing the compost into it to about 1cm ($\frac{1}{2}$ inch) below the rim. Then level off the surface and firm it down with your hand. Before you begin sowing, label each container. It is a good idea to put the date as well as the name of the seeds. Be sure to use a waterproof pencil.

The compost must be made moist before sowing; it should be neither dry nor waterlogged. Sow thinly to make pricking out easy. Very fine seed should not be covered with compost after sowing. Otherwise the rule is to cover the seed with a depth of compost roughly equal to its own diameter. The best way to sow is to tap the seed from the packet with your forefinger while moving your hand over the surface. To aid even distribution of very fine seed when sowing, mix the seed with a little silver sand. Large seed can be sown with the fingers or a pair of tweezers. If there is a lot of seed in a packet, there is no need to sow it all at once. Often sowings can be staggered over a couple of weeks or so. This will provide batches of plants in different stages of development, giving you longer flowering and cropping periods. After sowing, water-in the seed using a mist of water from a fine sprayer. The same technique should be used for subsequent waterings, and also, for watering the tiny seedlings when they show through. It is not a good idea to water by immersing the sowing containers in water, as is so often suggested, because this leaches out all the soluble fertilizers added to the seed compost. Overwatering must in fact be avoided since too much water can suffocate the seed – air must be able to penetrate for it to germinate. On the other hand, complete drying out once the seed has started to germinate is equally fatal.

GERMINATION AND AFTERCARE

After sowing, cover the seed container with a sheet of clean white paper, then lay a piece of glass on top or slide it into a polythene bag to help retain moisture; the paper prevents drips of condensation from saturating the compost surface and waterlogging the seed. Some greenhouse plant seed germinates best if exposed to a certain amount of light, which is all the more reason for not sowing too deeply. This is particularly worth doing with bromeliads, cacti and other succulents, calceolarias, rubber plants, gloxinias, lettuce, petunias, African violets and Cape primroses.

When the containers are put in a propagator be careful to check that the temperature is optimum for the seed type. Obviously, one must not try to germinate different types of seed with widely different temperature requirements at the same time. If the temperature is excessively high, although germination will be speeded up, pale, weak, lanky seedlings will be produced.

Most of the popular greenhouse-sown seed germinates in one to three weeks. Some may take considerably longer, so do be patient. As soon as germination is seen to be taking place, remove all covering. Pricking out and transferring to potting compost must be done as soon as the seedlings can be safely handled without damage. The sooner this is done after germination the less setback the seedling will suffer and the less likelihood there is of damaging the roots. The best tool for this job is a pair of long finely tipped tweezers but be careful not to actually grasp the seedlings with them. Just lift using the 'V' shape made by the tips of the tweezers. You can adjust the distance between the tips, according to seedling root size, by varying your finger pressure. Another popular tool for pricking out is a thin strip of wood or plastic with a 'V' notch cut at the end. If you need to handle a seedling with the fingers, lift it by one of the first formed 'seed leaves' and not by the stem. Replant the seedlings using a blunt-pointed dibber to make holes in the potting compost just large enough to take the roots easily.

Lift the seedling carefully from underneath when pricking out. Handle only the seed leaves.

The seedlings can be transferred to pots or to plastic seedling trays, depending on their further treatment. Many pot plants can initially be grown-on for a time in trays, which avoids the use of lots of small pots. To prevent damping-off (see page 56), water-in the seedlings with Cheshunt compound.

In the case of bedding plants, be particularly careful not to overcrowd seed trays. About 24 plants per tray is average. Seed, such as lobelia that yields crowds of minute seedlings, should be 'patched' out. This means lifting them in tiny groups and not attempting to separate out individual seedlings. The groups can be subsequently treated as a single plant and will grow as a clump perfectly well.

HARDENING-OFF

Before bedding plants are put out in permanent positions in the garden, they must be gradually acclimatized to full light conditions and low temperatures. If this is not done, and they are suddenly transferred from the warmth of the greenhouse, they will immediately become sickly and take a long time to start growing. Start hardening-off about two weeks before planting-out time which is roughly May–June, depending on area. If you are not sure about the timing, find out what the local parks or keen neighbouring gardeners do. The hardening-off procedure begins with moving the plants to the coolest part of the greenhouse, then, later, to closed unheated frames outside. Shade the frames from full sun at first but reduce the degree of shade or the period of shading each day. At the same time, give more and more ventilation until the plants are fully exposed. In the early stages, however, it may be necessary to close the frames at night if you think that there is any risk of frost.

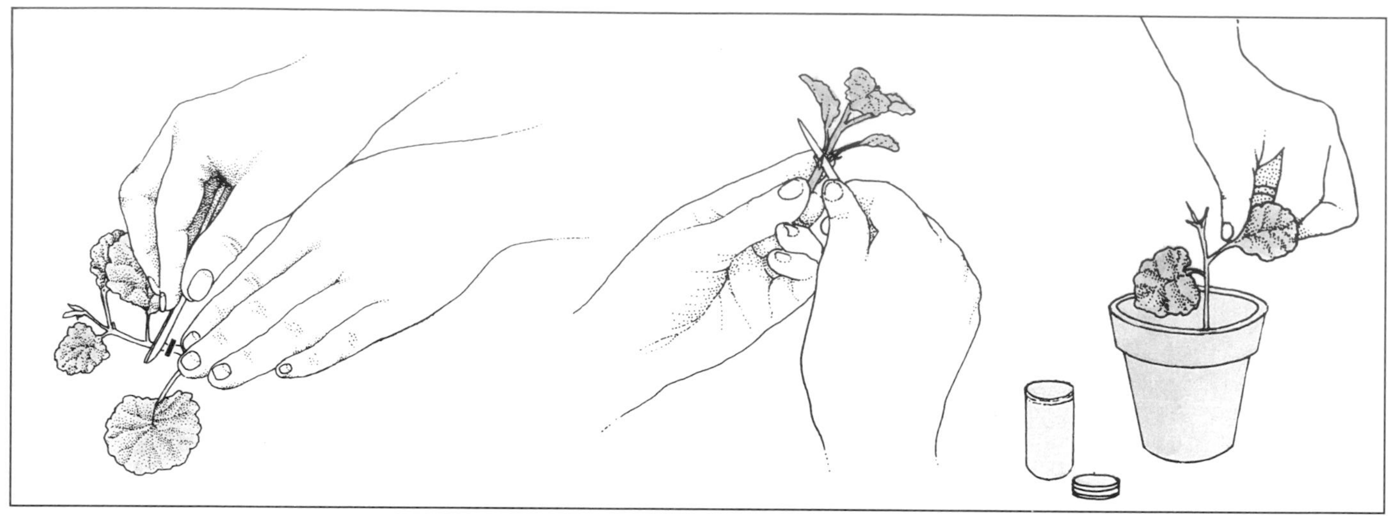

For a softwood cutting, cut off selected shoot with a sharp blade, pull away lower leaves and make a clean cut below nodes, dip stem in hormone rooting compound and insert in compost.

VEGETATIVE PROPAGATION

SOFTWOOD CUTTINGS

Cuttings taken from greenhouse plants are usually 'softwood', that is taken from soft immature growth. The best time to take cuttings is when the plants have just moved into their active growth period, as in spring. However, some cuttings can be taken in early autumn. Semi-hardwood and hardwood cuttings are cut from woody plants and shrubs. These can also be rooted in the greenhouse.

When taking cuttings, select small vigorous shoots – about a finger length is long enough. Use a sharp blade such as a razor, so not to bruise the tissue, and cut the shoot at the base of the stem, just below the point where the leaves are borne. The leaves, just above the cut, must then be pulled away. It is from this point that the roots will eventually emerge. The cutting is then inserted into a cutting compost consisting of a mixture of clean grit and peat. A proprietary cutting compost can also be used. Several cuttings may be inserted around the edge of a pot, but seed trays can be used instead if there are many cuttings to be rooted. Small bags, like mini growing bags, are available for rooting cuttings. Finally, put the cuttings where they will receive the correct amount of warmth and will not lose moisture during rooting. Covering the containers with clear sheet polythene or a polythene bag may be adequate, or use a covered propagator to provide extra warmth and maintain humidity.

You can dip the base of the cuttings in a hormone rooting preparation before insertion into the compost. This sometimes hastens rooting, and most of these preparations also contain a fungicide to prevent rotting. Some cuttings of greenhouse plants, such as nerium and tradescantia, root very easily just standing in water, for example. Others, such as camellia, take quite a time. The cuttings and the compost must not be allowed to dry out whilst rooting. The method known as 'mist propagation' automatically keeps cuttings sprayed with a fine mist of water to keep them at the point of maximum water uptake. Small units for this method are now available for the keen amateur. As soon as a reasonable root system has developed, the cuttings must be potted into a proper potting compost.

A very simple procedure for rooting cuttings without the aid of a propagator in summer and early autumn is to put a little cutting compost at the bottom of small polythene bags and insert the cuttings in this. The bags are then closed and hung up in the greenhouse. When rooting occurs it can be seen through the polythene.

LEAF CUTTINGS

This method can be used for a large number of favourite greenhouse plants, particularly for the gesneria and begonia families. It is especially applicable to plants with bold leaf veins. Leaf cuttings can be propagated in several ways. The simplest is to take a leaf and make slits with a razor blade in the veins at intervals on the undersurface. The leaf is then placed flat, slits downward, on the surface of some cutting compost. A few clean pebbles can be used, if necessary, to keep it flat and in close contact. Roots will grow from the slits and tiny plants form that can be separated and potted. Leaves can also be cut into small triangles with a vein at the apex of each triangle. The point with the vein is then inserted into the rooting com post in the same way as a stem cutting. If plants have elongate leaves these can usually be cut into sections, and each inserted in a similar manner. Some small-leaved plants, such as African violets and peperomias, can be propagated by merely detaching a leaf with a piece of stalk attached and inserting it as far as the top of the stalk in a rooting compost. Leaf cuttings usually need warmth, and the maintenance of humidity is essential.

DIVISION

This is the simplest and quickest way of propagation and can be done with any plants that form a clump of roots. First remove the plant from its pot, then, using a sharp knife, cut down through the clump to make several pieces. Pot each one in the usual manner. Division is best done with most plants just as growth is about to begin. Make sure the compost is moist, initially, but after potting be sparing with water until the plant is seen to be actively growing.

In the case of tuberous plants, division should be done after the tubers have started into growth, when well-defined shoots can be seen. Divide them up so that there's a shoot to each piece, then dust the cut surfaces with powdered charcoal to check sap loss before potting.

LAYERING

This method is used mainly for climbers and trailers but can sometimes be used for other plants if their stems are flexible enough. A length of stem is led into a pot of rooting compost so that a short portion is immersed. This is then weighted in position. You can either make a slit in the stem where it dips into the compost, or remove the leaves at that point, as with stem cuttings. When roots have formed, the stem is cut from the parent plant and potted into a potting compost.

Leaf cuttings: leaf with cut veins on underside and detached leaves with stalk in compost.

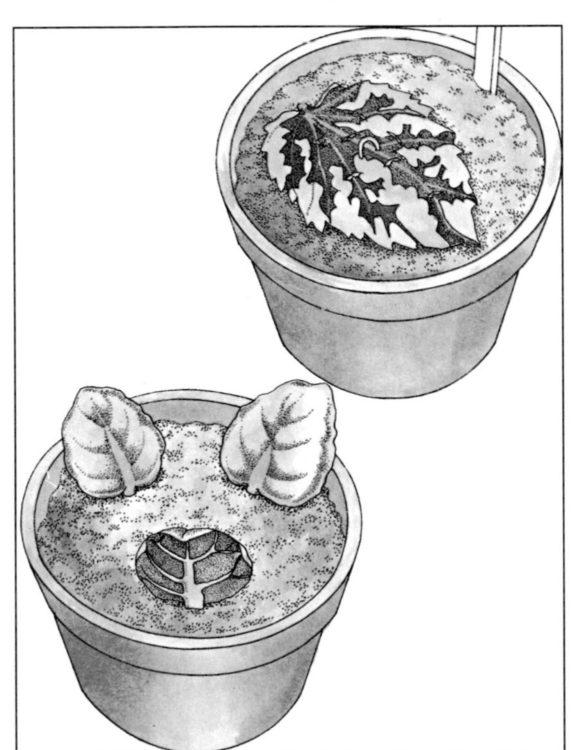

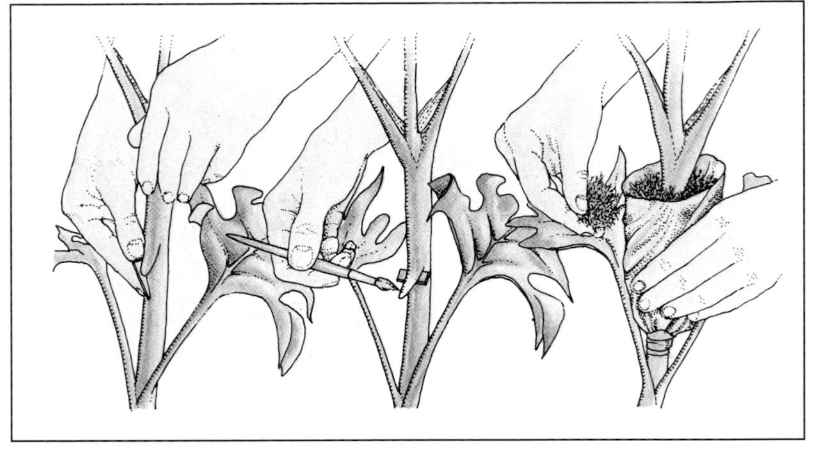

When air layering, cut an upwards slit, insert a wedge of peat dusted with hormone powder and enclose with clear polythene containing moist peat and moss.

AIR LAYERING

This can be useful for plants that become 'leggy' and lose their lower leaves. It is most applicable for plants such as the rubber plant (*Ficus elastica*). First make a slit in the stem where a new root system is required and insert a tuft of peat dusted with a hormone powder. Then fasten a ball of moist peat and sphagnum moss around the slit, wrap it around with clear polythene sheeting and secure with string or florists' wire. When roots can be seen through the polythene, cut the stem just below the point from which they emerge and pot in the usual way. Moderate warmth over several weeks is essential for the success of this method, so it is best to start it during late spring.

OFFSETS

Greenhouse bulbs and corms may produce small 'bulblets' around their sides as they reach maturity. These can be isolated and potted individually. Such small storage organs may take several years to become large enough to flower. Some rhizomes and tubers, such as achimenes and gloriosa, also reproduce themselves. The offspring can be separated during the dormant period and may flower well in the first year of potting.

Some plants, bromeliads, for example, send out shoots from the base which form into young plants. These can be carefully cut off close to the parent stem, which eventually dies, and potted separately.

Separate offsets from the base of bulbous plants when repotting and pot these individually.

HYGIENE, PESTS AND DISEASES

A high standard of hygiene is essential to successful greenhouse horticulture. The congenial environment you provide for your plants is also one in which pests and diseases thrive and quickly multiply, spreading from plant to plant. The greenhouse structure and all equipment must, therefore, be kept clean, and sickly plants must be kept apart from healthy ones.

Crude animal manures, unsterilized leaf mould and garden soil must never be brought inside. Dirty rainwater collected from roofs is another source of infection. The dangers of using the ground soil have been explained (see page 16).

Pots, seed trays, and other similar equipment must be kept clean, and preferably sterilized before use each year. Seed and potting composts should be stored in clean plastic bags or lidded plastic bins to keep them free from contamination.

Cleaning the interior of the greenhouse is essential for combatting pests and diseases, while a clean exterior admits maximum light.

GREENHOUSE STERILIZATION

The term 'sterilization' does not have the same implications as it does when used to describe an operating theatre, for example. The aim in the greenhouse is to destroy as many as possible of the pests and diseases which might overwinter there. These are frequently found in the form of eggs or fungal spores. For the home gardener only a limited number of disinfectants are available, for safety reasons. The most widely used are those based on phenol. These are relatively safe, provided they are used strictly according to the instructions on the label.

The best time to disinfect and clean your greenhouse is when all plants can be removed, preferably before the main growing season begins. Autumn to late winter is often most convenient. You should start by washing down the entire interior structure, glass and frame, with a soft brush soaked with the manufacturer's recommended dilution of the disinfectant. Apply the solution generously and make sure it gets into cracks and joints, and into the 'T' slots of alloy structures. The floor and staging should be soaked too.

After this treatment, leave the house closed for a couple of days, then open vents and allow a few days for vapours to clear. Although there is usually a persistent odour, as long as all plants are container grown they can be moved back in without fear of damage. If the ground soil is treated, a longer period of time must elapse before it can be used for growing. A test can be made by sowing some cress seed in samples of the treated soil. If this germinates and grows normally, the soil is safe to use.

The phenolic disinfectants will clear algae, slimes and mosses. There is also a disinfectant called Algofen that can be used for this purpose during the growing period since it's safe with plants. It's excellent for keeping automatic watering systems and capillary matting, for example, algae free and hygienic. It can also be used on the surface of potting composts.

Don't use your greenhouse to store junk. Clutter will provide hiding places for pests and diseases and make cleaning difficult. Keep the exterior of the greenhouse crystal clear in winter to admit maximum light. Also, try to keep the surroundings weed free at all times, particularly because many weeds can be hosts for invasive pests, whitefly, for example.

PESTICIDES AND THEIR USE

The most important point before buying or using pesticides is to *read the label*. Then always follow the instructions exactly. Some pesticides damage certain plants and should not be used near them. With regard to food crops, there are usually restrictions on how soon they can be picked after spraying. Always avoid personal contact in any form. Never store pesticides in unlabelled containers or domestic bottles, and *keep them out of reach of children*.

Sprays are generally more effective than pesticidal dusts but the most efficient contact method is fumigation, either with 'smokes' or aerosols. Systemic pesticides are also extremely efficient since they are absorbed by the plant, making all parts poisonous to the pest. They remain active for a long time but they are not initially as fast acting as contact methods. Always make sure that the undersurfaces of leaves get thorough treatment, since this is usually where pests and diseases first congregate. It is wise to make routine inspections of your plants every few days. A small magnifying glass is helpful to spot minute pests such as red spider mite and mould or mildew spots in the early stages. Act immediately if trouble is suspected. Treatment is usually easier and more effective in the early stages.

Pay particular attention to the underside of the leaves when spraying with a pesticide.

Lighting the fuse of a cone fumigator. Check that no plants need to be removed before its use.

COMMON PESTS AND DISEASES

ANTS

When large numbers of ants invade the compost in pots they cause considerable root disturbance and severe plant wilting. They usually get in via the drainage holes. Several specific antkiller dusts are now available which are very effective.

APHIDS

Greenfly are the most common aphids in the greenhouse but others frequently find their way in too. Like a number of similar insects, they deposit a sticky secretion called 'honeydew' on which an unsightly blackish mould grows. There are many aphid killers on the market and you should choose according to the plants you are growing.

Spraying tomato plants. Leave for specified time before picking.

DAMPING-OFF

This is a problem affecting seedlings after pricking out, and is caused by several fungi. It is common when unsterilized composts, garden soil or crude manures are used, and where hygiene is poor. It causes the seedlings to topple over and shrivel. The trouble can spread very quickly unless immediately checked. You should water with Cheshunt compound, available from garden shops. It is advisable to do this as a routine preventive measure after all pricking out.

EARWIGS

The presence of this pest should be suspected if flower petals or leaves are being eaten away and left with tattered and ragged edges. Seedlings can also be attacked. Earwigs hide during daylight and become active at night so the damage may seem something of a mystery. Plants with large flowers, such as chrysanthemums, are very susceptible. Pots stuffed with straw and inverted on canes can be used to trap the earwigs. An effective chemical that is safe for most plants, including food crops, is permethrin.

GREY MOULD (Botrytis cinerea).

This mould always appears sooner or later, even in the best kept greenhouses. It attacks both living and dead plant tissues, forming a greyish-to-brownish furry covering. It is frequently seen on damaged tissue. If the mould is disturbed, a smoke-like cloud of spores is released which spreads the infection. Pelargoniums, lettuces, and chrysanthemum flowers are often affected. On tomatoes the fungus causes small whitish rings with a tiny central black speck on the fruits (ghost spotting). The fruit is, however, safe to eat. The fungus is encouraged by generally bad hygiene, poor ventilation and excessive humidity. Fortunately, TCNB fumigation and spraying with a mixture of benomyl and a foliar feed (a proprietary formulation is available) can both prevent and control the fungus. It's wise to use them as a preventive measure.

LEAFMINER

This pest particularly affects chrysanthemums, and sometimes polyanthus. It manifests itself as wandering brownish lines on the foliage, and a tiny burrowing grub is responsible. It can be prevented and controlled by spraying with permethrin, pirimphos-methyl, or gamma-HCH.

MEALY BUG

This appears as tiny scales with a mealy, whitish waxy covering. It is common on succulents and thick-leaved plants. Wipe off by hand when possible, using a tuft of cotton wool saturated in methylated spirit. Where infestation is considerable spray with pirimphos-methyl.

MOULDS AND MILDEWS
There is a wide variety of these fungi. Most of them form whitish-to-greyish velvety coatings on foliage, usually appearing at first as isolated patches. They are encouraged by poor ventilation, overcrowding and cold damp conditions. There are now a number of general-purpose fungicides available, including systemic types, which effectively control a wide spectrum of these fungi. The black sooty mould which grows on insect secretions is not in itself harmful, merely unsightly, but it could interfere with plant metabolism. It is best to wipe it off using cotton wool soaked in a weak solution of detergent in water.

RED SPIDER MITE
This can be a very serious pest if allowed to gain a hold. It usually appears during the summer months. Foliage may turn yellowish and plants become sickly for no apparent reason. A look at the undersurface of the leaves through a powerful lens will reveal tiny spider-like greyish-to-red mites and spherical whitish eggs. In severe attacks they may swarm and form an obvious web, by which time the plants are usually ruined and are best burnt. Sterilization helps to prevent the pest and kills overwintering eggs. Probably the best treatment and control is fumigation at seven-day intervals with a pirimphos-methyl smoke cone.

SCALE INSECTS
These are similar to mealy bugs in habit and they attack similar plants, but they appear as cream-to-brownish scales without the mealy coating. They often cause a sooty mould on foliage just below where they congregate. Treatment is the same as for mealy bug.

SCIARID FLY MAGGOTS
These are tiny whitish-coloured maggots which attack roots and the base of plants and seedlings. They can do a surprisingly large amount of damage; wilting may be the first sign of their presence. They are the larvae of tiny flies, which may be noticed hovering nearby. Peat composts and damp conditions seem to encourage them. If possible, let pots become dryish and then water with pirimphos-methyl. The flies should be controlled by general fumigation with a general-purpose smoke cone.

SLUGS, SNAILS, WOODLICE
These common garden pests find their way into the greenhouse and cause severe damage. Just one snail or slug can eat a box of seedlings overnight. They hide during the day, under staging, for example. There are a number of baits available. The miniature pellets are particularly useful in the greenhouse. Woodlice eat roots and seedlings but are easily controlled with antkiller dusts.

THRIPS
These minute insects produce whitish patches surrounded by black specks on leaves. To confirm their presence, place white paper under the plant and shake the foliage. Wriggling insects will fall and show up clearly. Use a general systemic insecticide.

VIRUS DISEASES
Symptoms include yellowing and mottling of foliage, distortion, stunting, striping of flower colours, and general unsatisfactory growth. They can be spread by insects, pruning and cutting tools, and by handling. Plants should be burnt and not used for propagation. There's no cure.

WHITEFLY
This is a tiny fly with whitish triangular wings. It usually occurs in considerable numbers and, like aphids, causes sooty mould. Weeds around the greenhouse can harbour whitefly. Fumigate with special whitefly smoke cones.

*Scale insects (**left**) and whitefly (**right**), two common pests which both cause sooty mould.*

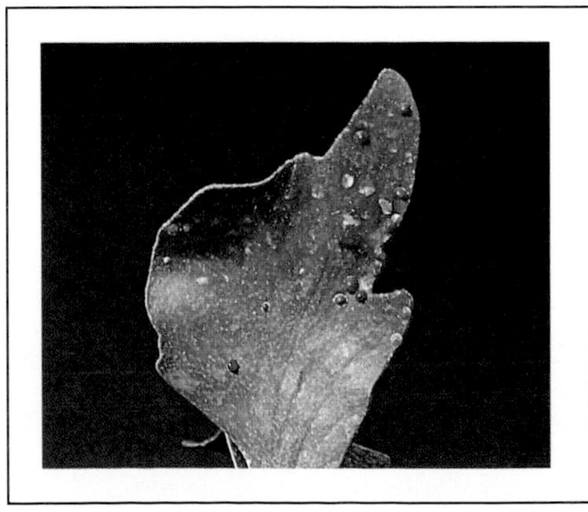

FLOWERS AND CROPS ALL YEAR ROUND

Some planning and organization is essential if you are to maximize the potential of your greenhouse. As already mentioned, the limitations or advantages of the site regarding light, shade and warmth, must be taken into account when you choose what to grow.

Once you have chosen the varieties, their positioning in the greenhouse is the next consideration. Those needing shade can be put under staging or under shrubby plants or climbers, or a part of the greenhouse can be deliberately shaded for them. Plants needing good light must be sited along the south side, where the greenhouse is not overshadowed and, if low growing, put on raised shelves. Those sensitive to chill must be set well away from doors or draughts. Conversely, those needing airy conditions can be placed near ventilators.

During summer, many plants like moderate humidity. To satisfy this need without raising humidity excessively in the whole greenhouse, group plants with similar requirements. You could stand those needing more humidity together on a surface of moist peat, shingle or on capillary matting, and use polythene sheeting screens to localize the higher atmospheric humidity. If you want to accommodate a wide range of plant types, partitions or screens can be used to divide off larger sections of the greenhouse so that several areas with different conditions and temperatures can be obtained.

Don't forget that you can use the greenhouse roof to support a variety of climbers. You should, however, avoid perennial types that need permanent positions as these make cleaning and sterilizing difficult if not impossible. Annuals, such as ipomoea, thunbergia and cobaea, are no problem, and can be cleared out at the end of the year. You can also use hanging-baskets or plastic pots with holes drilled in the rims and fitted with wires to display many lovely plants. These are indispensable items for the conservatory and give the greenhouse a professional touch.

Also, with careful planning it is surprising how wide a selection of plants can be grown. Flowering pot plants, cut flowers and vegetables can be fitted in, and even specialist subjects like orchids and chrysanthemums.

A greenhouse year, for example, can run as follows. In winter, if the greenhouse is kept frost free, winter salads, such as lettuce, and herbs, such as parsley and mint, can be grown most of the time. Using a frame with a soil warming cable for gentle forcing, beetroot, carrot, radish, salad onion and turnip can be added. (Being small, these also make useful 'catch crops' to fit alongside larger plants like tomatoes and sweet pepper, so utilizing space to the full.) In a warmed section under the staging, vegetables such as chicory, rhubarb and seakale can be forced and blanched. Potatoes can also be forced for Christmas if seed potatoes are sprouted and potted up in autumn.

Climbing French beans can be started early in the year and grown on where the tomatoes will follow. Along a south side is best. The bean crop has to be gathered over a very short period, and there should be plenty of time to set out the tomatoes. The tomatoes should continue to give fruit from about June to almost winter if the late weather is favourable. From late winter to spring, bedding plants can be raised together with many plants for later display in the greenhouse, con-

Position plants carefully to meet their needs and to maximize use of space.

servatory or home. This is also the time to start cucumbers, melons, sweet peppers and aubergines, all of which can be grown in the same greenhouse if carefully positioned and trained.

Most of the greenhouse ornamentals can be placed on or below staging, opposite the tomatoes and vegetables during summer. The tomatoes can be followed by chrysanthemums grown on outdoors during summer and moved inside in autumn. Cymbidium orchids can also be moved in and will give a wonderful show from late winter to spring. Pot plants, such as cineraria and calceolaria, sown in late summer should provide a dazzling show from Christmas onwards (some varieties make fine gifts), and hardy spring-flowering bulbs, potted in autumn, give added colour and interest.

There follows a detailed, month-by-month planner to help you organize your greenhouse year. Indoor cultivation has the obvious advantage over outdoor gardening that plans and routines are not interrupted by unfavourable weather.

With careful planning a wide variety of plants can be grown. In summer, ornamentals can be put on staging opposite tomatoes and vegetables.

Early in the year, a frost-free, unheated greenhouse gives adequate protection for many plants.

YEAR PLANNER

JANUARY

Sow lettuce and other salad vegetables. Begin sowings in the propagator of summer-autumn flowering pot plants and plants requiring long growing period, such as F1 hybrid geraniums. Some bulbs already in the plunge may be ready to bring in. Propagate chrysanthemums and carnations from cuttings. Sow freesias, seven seeds to each 130mm (5in) pot. Rhubarb can be brought in for forcing under the staging. Pot-on actively growing pot plants such as primulas, calceolarias and cinerarias. Be cautious with watering and ventilate freely if there is a mild spell. Keep the greenhouse glass clean.

FEBRUARY

Sow antirrhinums and fibrous-rooted begonias, if not done in January, and also more pot plants: thunbergia, schizanthus, salpiglossis, exacum, torenia and heliotrope, for example. Sow lilies, and pot-up scales which you have carefully detached from saved bulbs for propagation. Sow sweet peas and border plants, such as delphiniums, for later transfer to the garden. Sow Christmas cherry (*solanum*). Make more vegetable sowings including radish, peas and beetroot. Start dahlia tubers into growth. Sow vegetables for later transference to the outdoor plot. Late in the month, sow tomatoes for early crops. Prune vines, cutting back lateral growth to two eyes.

MARCH

The majority of bedding plants can now be sown. The sowings of some seed should be staggered over two-week intervals until end of April. Sow greenhouse plants which are extra-sensitive to cold such as Cape primroses, tuberous begonias, ipomoeas, gloxinias (F1 seed) and African violets (F1 seed). Sow cucumbers, sweet peppers, melons, aubergines, and cape gooseberries, and also tomatoes if not done in February. Sow plants for sub-tropical bedding, such as ricinus and ornamental maize. Many bulbs, corms, and tubers can be started into growth, for example, achimenes, smithiantha, gloxinia, gloriosa, caladium (for foliage), hippeastrum, polianthes (tuberose) and sprekelia. Some early sown tomatoes may be ready for permanent planting. Start fuchsias, geraniums and other pelargoniums, and any other perennial pot plants into growth that have been dormant over winter.

APRIL

Sow quick-maturing and warmth-loving bedding plants such as African and French marigolds and zinnias. Nemesia is also best sown now without artificial heat to get short sturdy plants. Be prompt with the pricking out now required, and water-in the seedlings with Cheshunt compound to avert damping-off. There should now be masses of flowers and colour from spring flowering pot plants and bulbs. Be careful not to let temperatures rise too high now that the sun is more powerful. Some shading may be essential to maintain cool conditions and prevent plants from wilting or fading quickly. Use Coolglass shading which can be wiped off later if necessary. Sow epiphyllums and other cacti and succulents. Take cuttings of stephanotis.

Sow peas in a trough in February and grow them in the greenhouse for an early crop.

Above *In May an unheated frame can be used for hardening-off bedding plants and others which have been grown in a heated greenhouse and are to go outside. In June replace these with any greenhouse pot plants being grown on or rested which do not need height.*

MAY

Sow cinerarias, calceolarias, and all pot plant primulas – if sown now some quick-flowering varieties may be ready for Christmas. All vegetable plants should now be in their final positions, and the canes or strings to train them set up. New plants brought in earlier as rooted cuttings, such as chrysanthemums, carnations and pelargoniums, should be potted on. Many plants saved from the last year will have made sufficient growth for cuttings to be taken. By about the middle of the month, bedding plants and others to go out later, should have the hardening-off treatment started. Keep a constant watch for pests.

JUNE

Over the next three months the sun's power can cause greenhouse temperatures to shoot up to a dangerous level for all plants. Most structures will need almost permanent shading. Damping down and watering must on no account be neglected. (Automatic systems for these can be set up.) Ventilation is also important, but don't let the wind rush through the greenhouse as this can cause serious damage. Early sown tomatoes should be cropping, and so should the all-female cucumber varieties, which are very prolific. Sow sub-tropicals such as the Abyssinian banana (*Musa ensete*), the bird-of-paradise flower (*Strelitzia reginae*) and palms. These need plenty of warmth in the early stages for germination and quick growth, but can be acclimatized to quite cool conditions later. Hardened-off bedding plants should now have been taken out of frames and replaced by greenhouse pot plants being grown on or rested, as long as they are not tall growing. This can save much space at a time when it's in great demand.

Below *During summer, watering several times a day may be necessary. Ideally, the compost should always be just moist, never dry nor waterlogged.*

JULY

Keep an eye on tomatoes to see that all is well with flowering, pollination and fruiting. Spray the flowers with a mist of water and/or shake the plants to distribute pollen. Water evenly and regularly so that the compost is always moist. Avoid temperatures over 27°C (80°F) whilst tomatoes are ripening. Keep cucumbers and melons properly trained and also moist, never wet. Many ornamentals require supports and/or training. Perpetual flowering carnations may need disbudding and also calyx menders if splitting is a problem. Large-flowered begonias should have the female buds (with winged seed capsule) removed at an early stage. Keep a special watch for red spider mite, especially if the weather is hot and dry. Many plants potted earlier may now have exhausted their potting compost and need feeding. Cyclamen corms can be started, convex side down, in 130mm (5in) pots, with their tops just above the compost. Place in shaded frames. Cuttings from many ornamentals can be taken, including pelargoniums.

Autumn is the time to pot and plunge spring-flowering bulbs. Avoid putting varieties which flower at different times in the same bowl.

Flowering pot plants, such as these red begonias, make an eye-catching display during summer months.

AUGUST

Continue to take cuttings when they become available. Melons in the ripening stage should be watered more sparingly but not allowed to dry out. Pot up nerine greenhouse hybrids, but not the garden forms, one to a 130mm (5in) pot. Pot arums and also lachenalias, which may flower around Christmas time; keep them cool. Chrysanthemums standing outdoors should be protected from possible wind damage and checked for pests and diseases, especially leafminer. Feeding, generally, must be continued and be punctilious with the dead-heading of flowers as they fade, to prolong blooming. Hardy annuals can be sown now for overwintering in the greenhouse and early colour in spring.

SEPTEMBER

This is usually the time to clean and tidy up. Any plants past their best, looking sickly or scruffy, should be critically assessed and discarded if necessary. The house should be cleared of fallen leaves, flowers, plant debris and any weeds that have managed to get in during the summer. Plants that have been grown-on in frames can be brought in. Decoratives, such as nerium and callistemons, that have been standing outside for summer must also be put under cover, depending on weather conditions but before the first frosts. Check all pots are clean and free from soil pests, and all plants for health. Begin potting hardy bulbs and put them in the plunge. Leave tulips for next month. Sow salpiglossis for flowering next spring, also butterfly flower (*Schizanthus*) of which the large-flowered varieties are best for sowing now. Tomatoes that have ceased useful production can be cleared to make way for chrysanthemums. Ornamentals, such as calceolaria and cineraria, may need potting-on. Sow suitable lettuce varieties for winter-spring cropping, such as 'Dandie', 'Kloek', 'Kwiek', 'May Queen' and 'Sea Queen'.